Rosedale

THE EIGHTEENTH CENTURY COUNTRY ESTATE

OF

GENERAL URIAH FORREST

CLEVELAND PARK, WASHINGTON, D.C.

Louise Mann-Kenney

Washington, D.C.

1989

This publication was sponsored by Youth for Understanding International Exhange and published with grants from the Queene Ferry Coonley Foundation, Inc. and Uriah Forrest descendants.

Copyright © 1989 by Louise Mann-Kenney. All Rights Reserved.

Printed in the United States of America.

Library of Congress Catalog Card No. 89-060733

ISBN 0-9623591-0-6

Drawing by Marion Lane

Here in this country, instead of palaces, temples, tombs, or cathedrals, the real historical monuments are the fine old homes that tell the history of our American People. They keep a personal and appealing record of the way people lived when the nation was young.

—Richard Pratt, *A Treasury of American Homes*

Contents

Illustrations ... vi

Preface ... vii

Acknowledgments ... x

Chapter

I. The Origins of Rosedale
   A Sylvan Summer ... 1

II. The Building of Rosedale
   Forrest Additions, Interior and
   Exterior Furnishings ... 13

III. Landholder, Bankrupt, Clerk of Court
   Rosedale Saved ... 31

IV. Uriah Forrest's Final Years ... 41

V. Rosedale after Forrest ... 47

Sources and Notes ... 63

Index ... 81

Illustrations

Cover: Rosedale Entrance and Grounds. (National Cathedral School for Girls)

Frontispiece: Epigraph, Richard Pratt; Rosedale Drawing, Marion Lane. (Faulkner Family Collection)

Figures

1. Uriah Forrest, 1786-87	opposite page 1
2. Forrest-Marbury House, ca. 1865; Insert, Forrest House, ca. 1788	3
3. The Cottage, Pretty Prospects; Floor Plan	10
4. Rosedale, Southwest Corner and Facade	12
5. Rosedale from Above, West; Current Floor Plan	14
6. Sotterley Mansion	18
7. Rose-colored Bowl	20
8. Lavender Wedgwood Pitcher	20
9. Mahogany Dining Table	22
10. Mahogany Breakfast Table	24
11. French Clock	24
12. Tobacco Box and Silver Spoon	25
13. Side Chairs and Silk Samplers	25
14. Uriah Forrest's Desk	26
15. Rebecca's Bible and Silver Goblet	27
16. Quern Stepping Stone	29
17. Original Terrace, Rosedale	29
18. Uriah Forrest's Will	43
19. Rebecca Forrest In Maturity	46
20. Georgetown Home of Rebecca Forrest	48
21. Mr. and Mrs. John Green	50
22. President Cleveland's Country House, Red Top	52
23. Mrs. Cazenove Lee at Red Top Site	52
24. St. Alban's Wooden Church, 1896	53
25. Mrs. Avery Coonley with Family and Friends, Rosedale	58
26. Site Plan, Rosedale, Late Twentieth Century	60
27. Bronze Statue of Pan at Herb Cottage at the Cathedral	62

Preface

The purpose of this monograph is to establish by documentation the historic identity of Rosedale, an eighteenth-century country estate, and the life-style of the owner-builder, General Uriah Forrest and his family. It is a study that has not been done before. Previous writings have consisted of a mixture of local lore, family memorabilia, and records often inaccurately interpreted.

Diverse personal and professional reasons compelled me to undertake this task. As a history buff with family roots in colonial Virginia and Maryland, relics of the American past have always piqued my curiosity. As a longtime resident of the District of Columbia's community of Cleveland Park, located within the former boundaries of Rosedale, I have cherished memories of the old house and its acreage. The grounds were always open to respectful visitors. The secluded parklike setting and the quiet dignity of the estate were a haven—a welcome respite from the burgeoning city and its pedestrian and vehicular traffic.

I remember when the open space on the west side of the estate, the corner of 36th and Newark streets, was a touch football, softball, and frisbee field for young and old. The orange and gold leaves of the large maple in the center of that field were a fountain of color and beauty each fall. I recall the verdant peaceful quiet and the canopy of towering hickory, elm, and oak beyond the play area.

A less sentimental reason for this study was the awareness that the history of the Forrest family and the house and grounds was inadequate. There had been a litany of so-called facts repeated through the years that served as a history, but there was a paucity of primary sources and documentation. There were contradictions, gaps, and unanswered questions.

This realization crystallized during my participation in a seminar in historic preservation directed by Dr. Theodore Turak at American University in the fall of 1975. The purpose of the seminar was to investigate and record the social and architectural history of Cleveland Park. My responsibility was to assist the study by preparing the community for the project and by locating the sources available for research.

It was soon obvious that while there was ample material for a documented study of the development of the Victorian neighborhood, there were few sound sources available for a predevelopment history. Primary documentation of public and private records of the eighteenth to the mid-nineteenth centuries is generally limited. Records were often post facto recollections or were lost or destroyed by the ravages of nature and man. And because this was a new and changing country, records were scattered throughout several jurisdictions.

Restricted by time, the seminar reported primary data for the development of the neighborhood with selected reasonable secondary sources for its predevelopment period.

Challenged by this experience, I made a personal commitment at the conclusion of the seminar to undertake a search for documentation on the history of Uriah Forrest—purported first resident of the area—and the Rosedale estate. It was a difficult task, for the lifetime of the Forrests spanned the years before the Revolution to the early years of the Republic when, as has been noted, record keeping was of secondary importance.

There followed a program of lengthy and intensive research, conducted part time between professional obligations. Public and private records were examined. With no Forrest diary and few personal letters available, diaries and correspondence of eighteenth-century contemporaries, journals and writings of the period, and hearsay and family recollections were used as clues and cross-referenced to balance against historical fact.

By this process myths were dispelled. For example, Colonel Uriah Forrest did not lose his leg in either the battle of Brandywine or the battle of Germantown, as has been written. He fought in both engagements, and he was seriously wounded at Germantown when an enemy musket ball fractured his thigh. The fracture did not heal, and an amputation was performed more than a year later by an army surgeon from Baltimore who was sent to St. Mary's County where Forrest was on convalescent leave.

Nor is there any proof in military records or the meticulous collections of George Washington's writings that Uriah Forrest was an aide-de-camp to General George Washington during the war. He served under Washington's command in a special forces unit, and he was a trusted assistant during the founding of the Federal City. The president thought well of him and gave him an engraved silver goblet as a token of friendship and appreciation.

Forrest's famed dinner for President George Washington and "the Commissioners and others," recorded in Washington's diary March 29, 1791, was not held at Rosedale but at Forrest's home in Georgetown. Unreliable information, such as the above, has either been excluded from this monograph or, if included, has been labeled as such. Forrest's birthdate has been excluded because of the unreasonable time discrepancy—from 1746 to 1757—found among available sources.

With myths discounted, real people emerged, often with more substance and significance than previously thought. Research results have been rewarding and have proved substantial enough for the present monograph and a yet-to-be-published biography of Uriah Forrest. Investigation confirmed Rosedale to be an architectural monument worthy of its landmark status and a residence with a documentable social history that illuminates the pages of past regional studies.

Uriah Forrest, on the other hand, was discovered to have been more than a military hero and a founder of the Federal City; he was a man of national and international importance. He was not only an eyewitness to the turbulent times in which he lived but an active participant in the dramatic evolution of his country. In spite of his handicap, he was a privateer, a prosperous merchant, an effective state and national official, a wealthy landowner and builder. A self-made man, a friend to presidents, Forrest was often a mediator in political disputes of national significance and a courier of classified information between his government and foreign nations.

He surmounted personal catastrophes with courage—the loss of his leg because of the war, and, years later, the loss of his fortune, as a result of the economic panic of 1797 which led to his bankruptcy by 1802.

As with many histories of early America, questions remain. There are, however, multiple notes, sources, and cross-references furnished to facilitate the reader's understanding and to encourage further research on the "fine old homes" that Richard Pratt suggests are our "real historical monuments," and the "way people lived when the nation was young."

It is especially meaningful to me to be able to publish this study as the bicentennial year of the founding of the Federal City approaches.

Acknowledgments

Many individuals and organizations helped in various ways during this research project. I would like to thank the following: my earliest assistant, as she called herself, Mrs. Waldron (Elizabeth) Faulkner, who provided enthusiasm, support, and pertinent information; Miss Ann Forrest Matthews and Mrs. Elizabeth Matthews Black, great-great-granddaughters of Uriah Forrest, for their time, patience, and material assistance; Mrs. Margaret King Fresco, great-great-grandniece of Uriah Forrest, for her continuous contribution of information throughout this task; and all Forrest and Faulkner descendants who participated; the staff of Youth for Understanding, especially John Richardson, William Woessner, William Porter, and Max Darrow; the staff at Sotterley Mansion, particularly Marian Veitch, Lizette Day, Donna Ely, and Edward Knott for their helpfulness and hospitality.

The administrators, curators, and librarians of collections from Pennsylvania to Virginia who helped locate indispensable bits and pieces to weave this story together: John D. Kilbourne, Society of the Cincinnati; Eleanor Kubeck, National Cathedral School for Girls; Robert Lyle, Georgetown Library; Virginia Steele Wood, Library of Congress; Gary Scott and Barry Mackintosh, National Park Service; Jane Sween, Montgomery County Historical Society; Linda Stanley, Historical Society of Pennsylvania.

The staff of the following collections: Colonial Dames, Columbia Historical Society, Daughters of the American Revolution, and Martin

Luther King Library, Washington, D.C.; Lloyd House, Alexandria, Virginia; Maryland Historical Society, Baltimore, Maryland; St. Mary's County Historical Society, Leonardtown, Maryland.

I am indebted to those who shared their original research in related areas for this undertaking, including Janice Artemel, archaeologist-historian; Mary T. Arthur, researcher; William Buchanan, historian; George Gerber, preservationist; Dr. C. M. Harris, editor of *The Papers of William Thornton;* Priscilla McNeil, historian; Malcolm Vosburgh, researcher.

Deserving special mention are three who read this manuscript in whole or in part and made constructive and helpful suggestions: Dorothy Provine, Washington, D.C. Archives; Dr. George Callcott, Department of History, University of Maryland; and Dr. Dennis Gale, Center for Washington Area Studies, George Washington University, Washington, D.C.

I thank Cissel Gott Collins for her design and production contributions, Ann Hofstra Grogg for her perceptive copy editing, and photographer Henry Leonhardt for his sensitivity and professionalism. And finally, I thank my family for their patience and understanding support throughout this prolonged project.

LIEUT COL URIAH FORREST
Member of the Continental Congress

Uriah Forrest

Fig. 1. *Lieut Col. Uriah Forrest, Member of the Continental Congress, 1786-87, Philadelphia, Pennsylvania, with Forrest's signature.* Nineteenth-century engraving by Max Rosenthal after the original eighteenth-century oil on canvas by an unknown artist. The title on the engraving is incorrect. Military records confirm that Uriah Forrest was a full colonel in the Continental Army by 1781. (Collection of Library of Congress; background information courtesy Historical Society of Pennsylvania)

CHAPTER I

The Origins of Rosedale
A Sylvan Summer

Rosedale, the frame farmhouse Uriah Forrest built as a residence for himself and his family, 1793-94, stands today as a memorial to him and a reminder of the period in which he lived. Forrest, a war hero and amputee, a public official, and an original proprietor of the Federal City of Washington, D.C., constructed his home in what was considered rural Montgomery County, Maryland.

Rosedale sits on the crest of a hill, on the northwest portion of a conglomerate of colonial land patents, several miles north of Georgetown. Named to the National Register of Historic Places in 1973, Rosedale has become the symbolic heart of the District of Columbia's community of Cleveland Park, which developed around it in the late nineteenth and twentieth centuries.

The house is a modest structure so far as historic monuments go. Infrequently celebrated or protected, it has served as a residence during the nearly two hundred years of its existence. Despite the stresses of time, use, and periodic neglect, Rosedale has survived, and with a perseverance and stamina that mirror the character of the owner-builder, Uriah Forrest.

Rebecca and Uriah Forrest of Rosedale were natives of St. Mary's County, Maryland. They had been friends and neighbors since childhood. Both were fourth-generation Americans whose forebears were among the first English settlers of Tidewater Maryland. After their marriage, the Forrests moved inland from war-weary St. Mary's to seek a safer and more productive way of life.

The couple's lengthy courtship, as described by their granddaughter Maria Green Devereux, was a tender and devoted romance that flourished despite the disapproval of Rebecca's mother, who preferred that her daughter marry a man of wealth and position. Rebecca Plater Forrest was the eldest child of Tidewater aristocrats, wealthy heiress Elizabeth Rousby Plater and the honorable George Plater III, the sixth governor of Maryland. A petite raven-haired beauty with fine features and large gray eyes, gentle and reserved, Rebecca was well educated by tutors at Sotterley Manor, her family home. Uriah Forrest was the second and most adventurous son of Henrietta Raley Forrest, daughter of a respectable pioneer family, and Thomas Forrest, a successful middle-class planter. Handsome and debonair, Uriah, although informally educated, was literate, well read, and knowledgeable.

During the Revolutionary War, Forrest fought as an officer of Maryland's famed Flying Camp, a special unit that served directly under General George Washington. In the Battle of Germantown, 1777, Forrest suffered a severe fracture of his leg from an oversized British musket ball. He was evacuated to St. Mary's County to convalesce, but the wound did not respond to treatment. His leg was amputated at mid-thigh in November 1778.

On crutches because prostheses were crude and unsuitable for an amputation such as his, the retired colonel nonetheless participated fully in the post-Revolutionary enthusiasm for free enterprise. He formed the consignment merchant firm of Forrest & Stoddert, complete with a fleet of sailing vessels and offices in London, Bordeaux, Annapolis, and Georgetown.

Before ongoing international crises interrupted Forrest's lucrative mercantile trade, he had accumulated a fortune. When he abandoned his European headquarters and returned home, Mrs. Plater consented to his marriage to her daughter Rebecca. They were wed on October 11, 1789, at Sotterley. Shortly after the nuptials, Uriah Forrest left Sotterley to relocate his business on the north bank of the Potomac River at Georgetown and to establish a residence for his bride. Georgetown, founded in 1751 and peopled largely by merchants of Scottish descent, was a thriving inspection and shipping station for tobacco, the most important crop in the Tidewater.

On a bluff overlooking the Potomac River at Falls and Frederick streets (M and 34th), Forrest & Stoddert built an impressive Georgian brick town house for the first Forrest residence, now known as the Forrest-Marbury House (fig. 2). Rebecca remained at Sotterley until their first child, Elizabeth, was born, August 6, 1791, after which she

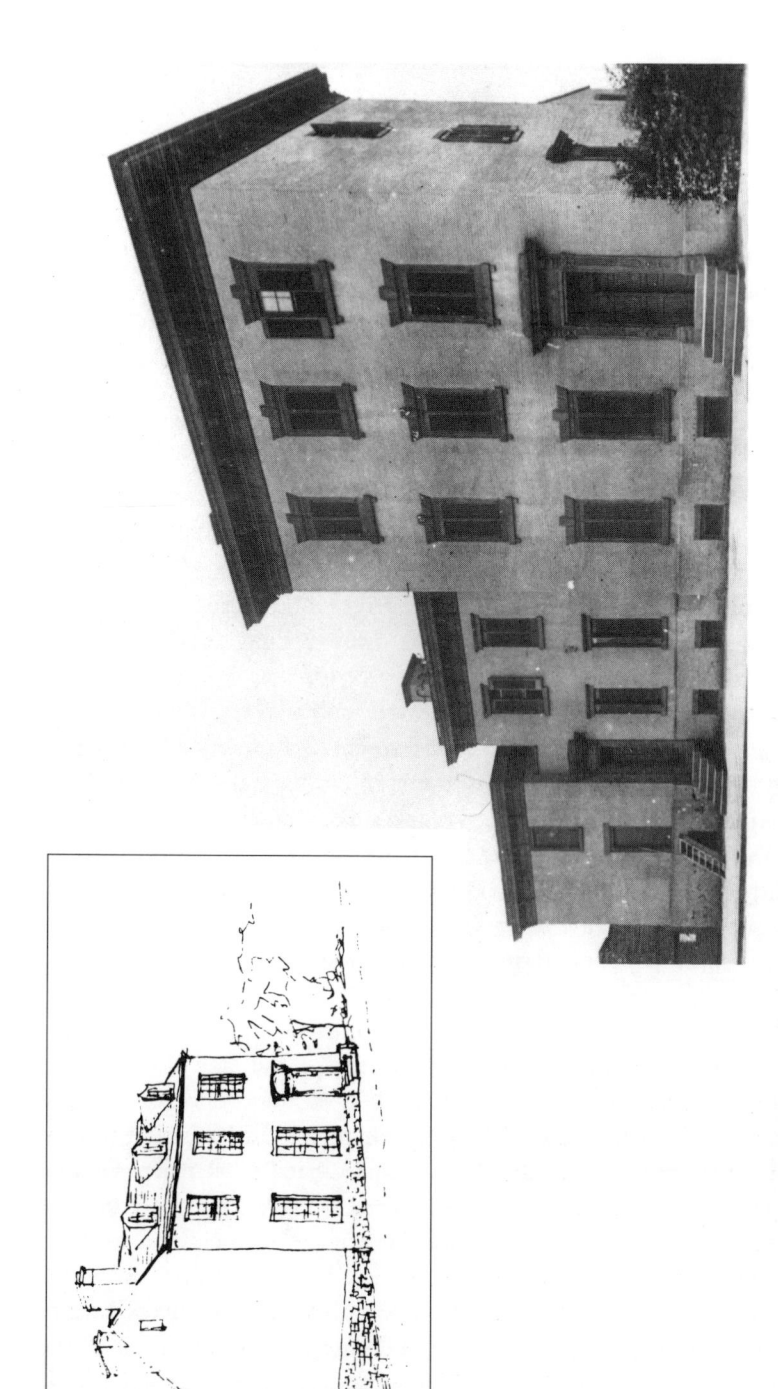

Fig. 2. *Forrest-Marbury House*, ca. 1865. Nineteenth-century additions to original Forrest House at Falls and Frederick Streets (M and 34th) Georgetown. (Collection of Library of Congress); insert, *Forrest House*, Georgetown, ca. 1788. (Courtesy Forrest-Marbury House Associates)

joined her husband in Georgetown.

For a variety of understandable reasons, Rebecca was not happy in the bustling port city. Primarily, she loved the countryside and horticulture. At Sotterley Manor, a large plantation that had belonged to her family for three generations, she had been free to enjoy the formal and informal gardens, the vast meadows, the spacious planted fields, and the secluded inlets and tributaries of the Patuxent River and nearby Chesapeake Bay. Although the Sotterley dock was active—a major point of entry for Tidewater commerce—the atmosphere was rural. There was sufficient space and refinement of business procedures for private, peaceful family living.

The location of the Forrest house in Georgetown was in sharp contrast. It was not private; indeed it was almost public, a step away from a busy town and harbor. It fronted directly on a main thoroughfare (Falls Street) next to a short rolling road (Frederick Street) that led to Forrest & Stoddert's waterside warehouse and wharf, adjacent to John Mason's chain-operated public ferry.

After congressional passage of the so-called Residence Bill on July 16, 1790, authorizing the establishment of a national capital, and the presidential decision the following year to survey "the ten mile square on both sides of the river Potomac . . . to comprehend Georgetown in Maryland and extend to the Eastern Branch" as a potential site, Georgetown grew rapidly. It served as headquarters for the Federal City building project with its attendant population increase, stage coaches, ferries, taverns, and public lot sales. Forrest's house was the center for his multiple business and civic pursuits as mayor of Georgetown, a delegate to the Maryland Assembly, and a proprietor of the capital city-to-be.

The Forrest house and nearby Suter's Tavern are together honored as the birthplace of the Federal City, for there the final negotiations for the acquisition of property for the national capital took place. George Washington noted in his diary on Tuesday, March 29, 1791, that he "dined at Colo. Forrest's to day with the Commissioners and others." The dinner, which in those days was served between one and three o'clock in the afternoon, preceded an evening meeting at Suter's Tavern. The next day's diary entry recorded the successful conclusion of the negotiations stating that all parties had mutually agreed to share their land "within bounds which were necessary for the [federal] city."

The port of Georgetown became a boom town, convenient for men of business but crowded and unsanitary for their wives and children. Mrs. Benjamin Stoddert, wife of Uriah Forrest's shipping partner, whose residence was Halcyon House on Prospect Street, did not find Georgetown to her taste. She spent much of her time in the cultured city of Philadelphia. Other families established country homes in nearby counties to escape the rigors of city life.

Moreover, by the spring of 1793, Georgetown had become a potential military target. With the French declaration of war against Great Britain, Spain, and Holland on February 1, 1793, America's coastal areas and waterways, major commercial routes for the warring powers, were in jeopardy and placed on alert. American coastlines and inland ports were as vulnerable as they had been during the War for Independence, as the Crown retaliated against its declared enemies as well as the renegade pro-French American privateers.

The same year the citizenry of Maryland, who had repeatedly chosen Forrest as a delegate to the Maryland Assembly in Annapolis, elected him a representative to the Third Congress of the United States, 1793-95, which met in Philadelphia. Forrest's legislative duties required frequent absences from his family. The combination of circumstances made it an excellent time for Rebecca to explore a safe haven for herself, toddler Elizabeth, and the new baby Benjamin Stoddert Forrest, born October 22, 1792. The haven she found was to become Rosedale.

According to family histories, the story of Rosedale began in the spring of 1793, when Rebecca Plater Forrest left the Forrest house for a respite in the peaceful pastoral environment of Pretty Prospects, the rural acreage that Uriah Forrest, Benjamin Stoddert, and William Deakins, Jr., jointly purchased in 1792. She settled there with her children in a small stone dwelling. A spring and summer in this bucolic setting convinced her that this was the place she would prefer to live and raise her family. Here, it was decided, the Forrests would build their permanent home, retaining the stone dwelling in the rear.

The little house on Pretty Prospects proved an ideal refuge for Rebecca and her youngsters that first summer. Situated in a lovely area, at the northwest corner of the extensive tract, it was secluded and unspoiled. Not too remote or primitive, it was a few miles from Georgetown, accessible on its western boundary by the old Georgetown to Frederick Road (Wisconsin Avenue) and on the east by the then-navigable waters of Rock Creek. The land had been cultivated by planters and millers since the early eighteenth century, some of whose families were still in residence nearby.

The location was legendary, recognized as such by Pierre L'Enfant the year before the Pretty Prospects purchase. "The heights from beyond Georgetown absolutely command the whole," he wrote Thomas Jefferson on March 11, 1791. In 1793, James Kent, a visitor from New York, noted on the margin of Tobias Lear's map that he had dined at the Forrest house on the hills about two miles north of Georgetown where there was "a fine view over the city and down the river."

The view was extraordinary. Through the heavily forested, oak-filled slopes, cleared of underbrush by earlier occupants, one could see the countryside, the cascading waters of the wide and deep Rock Creek, the port of Georgetown, and the shimmering river of the Potomac.

The topography and the accompanying natural plant life were a study in variations. Elevations ranged from 40 to more than 300 feet above sea level. The cottage rested on the highest point, a geological terrace of the piedmont plateau, where the air was clear and healthful. The lowest points were the fall line of Rock Creek on the east and the coastal plain of the Potomac River bed on the south.

Picture-perfect mountain growth—laurel and rhododendron—thrived at the higher elevations; marsh fern and jack-in-the-pulpit grew profusely in the lowlands. In between were undulating meadows of wild flowers, entangled with an abundance of rambling roses.

There was a diversity of mineral deposits—granite outcroppings, soapstone-laden gullies, and creek banks of clay, loam, and sand. The water supply was excellent, for the property was criss-crossed by freshets and streams. This was ancient land, its attributes known and appreciated from prehistory to the present. Here artifacts of nomadic Indian bands, dating from 10,000 B.C., as well as the later sedentary woodland tribes and the transitional "soapstone culture," have been uncovered.

Pretty Prospects and the surrounding area were dotted with geologically famous quarries of soapstone or granite—along today's

Connecticut Avenue at Albemarle Street, on the site of the Uptown Theater and the National Zoological Park (National Zoo), and on the grounds of the Naval Observatory near Massachusetts and Wisconsin Avenues. The quarries furnished the Indians with stone for fashioning weapons, tools, and utensils, and early settlers and the Federal City with building materials.

When the settlers displaced the Indians, portions of this beautiful resource-rich area were divided, patented, and, all too often, inaccurately surveyed. As original grantees or their heirs wished to sell their land, major errors—such as cloudy titles and overlapping grants—were discovered. Disputes were commonplace when property lines were subjected to the scrutiny of resurveys for sale purposes.

Pretty Prospects offers a good example of such problems. Sources vary, but they generally agree that around 1668 a large land grant was made to Henry Darnell, a prominent Marylander and friend of Lord Baltimore. The grant of thousands of acres extended from the Potomac River northward into what was to become Montgomery County. In 1703 Ninian Beall, an ambitious Scot and former indentured servant, patented 795 acres of that grant.

Beall named this 795 acres, beginning opposite the Little Falls of the Potomac and including both sides of Rock Creek, the Rock of Dumbarton. A resurvey in 1713 reduced his tract to 407 acres. To increase his father's grant, son George purchased an additional 1,380 acres in the same vicinity, appropriately named the Addition to the Rock of Dumbarton, plus a small adjacent tract called Beall's Lot. Portions of these properties, as well as the Gift, owned by Samuel Beall, Jr., Lucky Discovery, and other subdivisions were to become part of Pretty Prospects. In the meantime, new counties were created, their lines drawn and redrawn—changes that would complicate property transfers for years to come.

The survey of parts of these combined tracts for the new owners—Forrest, Stoddert, and Deakins—in 1793 ascertained their total acreage as 1,282 1/4, rather than the more than 2,000 expected. The land was renamed Pretty Prospects, and the deed was recorded in Stoddert's name alone for convenience.

The bounds of Pretty Prospects as recently researched by Priscilla McNeil are roughly these: northern boundary—Melvin Hazen Park, plus a northeast appendage that is part of Linnean Hill; eastern boundary—the National Zoo and part of Georgetown's P Street; southern boundary—Guy Mason Center, almost to Wisconsin Avenue, and that branch of Rock Creek north of Montrose Park. The western boundary, generally, was Wisconsin Avenue.

Although it is often written that Uriah Forrest was the first documented resident of what became the community of Cleveland Park, there had, in fact, been at least three owners of record of Forrest's share of Pretty Prospects prior to the Forrest, Stoddert, and Deakins purchase. Land records of 1765 list assets of earlier owners as "buildings, improvements, profits, commodities, advantages and appurtenances thereunto belonging." Much of the land the partnership purchased had been inhabited by owners or tenants. For example, that part of Beall's property which included Rock Creek from the Potomac River north to Pierce's Mill had been improved with at least seven structures in addition to a mill house, millstones, tools, and stocks of firewood.

Since there were buildings on the acreage Forrest selected and it was customary to use habitable buildings wherever possible, it is assumed that the cottage to which Rebecca and her children came in the spring of 1793 was already on the site. The antiquity of the stone structure further suggests that it predated the Forrest presence. Tradition dates the construction as 1740. Evaluations of the architectural style, materials, and construction by twentieth-century experts confirm that the cottage could have been on the premises very early in the eighteenth century. The cottage was probably one of the pre-1765 buildings included in the land records.

The building date may never be scientifically authenticated, for engineers warn that the fragility of the wood flooring and the joining mortar in the stone walls discourages further extensive examination. The cottage's antiquity and historical significance are, however, indisputable. It is the only stone residence of its kind extant in the Washington area and appears to have been built before the more sophisticated, two-story 1764-65 Old Stone House in Georgetown, reputedly the oldest house in the District of Columbia.

The design and construction of the cottage are practical and sturdy. Not a temporary shelter, it is a domestic unit, possibly the home of a planter, miller, or woodsman. The walls are thick and strong, made of local stone, irregular in size and shape, uncoursed, and joined with rubble mortar containing limestone and sand. The overall dimensions vary but are approximately 43 feet by 22 to 24 feet. Small and compact, the structure stylistically embodies the charming rusticity of a seventeenth-century English country cottage.

Traditionally known as "the cottage," the abode is actually two cottages, joined as one (fig. 3). The north section appears to be the original, with a later addition on the south. In almost every respect the style and use of materials in the north section are cruder and less refined than those of the south section. The exterior clearly shows the difference. The two roofs merge unevenly. The dimensions of the addition are wider on the east side by more than one foot, with the discrepancy accommodated for by a wall projection outward. Inside, a curved semihall with a doorway and a single step up connects the two uneven units to make a comfortable five-room residence.

The windows and doors, asymmetrically placed, further distinguish the two sections. The north section's windows and doors are set squarely into the stone walls and finished by slightly rounded corners in the mortar. The south section's windows and doors are inset equally, but trimmed above by an arch of single bricks vertically embedded in the mortar.

Six windows of differing sizes compose the fenestration. There is a door on the east in the north section, with the remnants of an archaic well nearly 30 feet away in the side yard. On the west side of the south section is another exterior door.

There are two large brick fireplaces—one for each cottage—joined back to back. The first fireplace is large and rudimentary, with a stepped-back brick mantel. The second is nearly flush in a brick wall, with the opening trimmed at the top by the same vertically inserted brick arch seen on the exterior windows. The arch above the fireplace is composed of a double row of vertical bricks, a trim repeated above the small baking oven beside the main opening.

Another major difference between the two cottages is the support and partition system. Rough-hewn tree trunks, aligned north-south, serve as post and horizontal beam supports for the north section. The

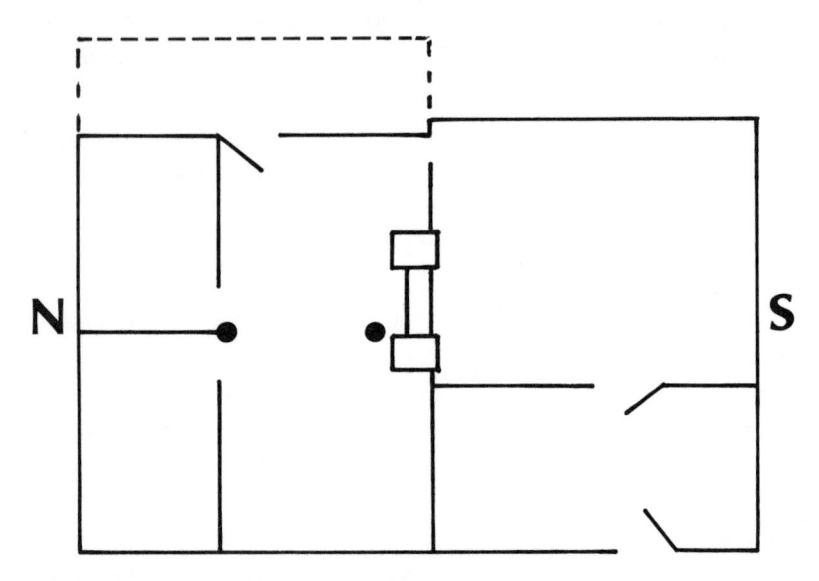

Fig. 3. *The Cottage, Pretty Prospects.* (Photograph by Max Darrow, Youth for Understanding); *Floor Plan.* (By author)

interior is divided into three parts—a main room and two small sleeping rooms, arranged east-west and separated by random-width board partitions. The south section, more thoughtfully planned, utilizes a brick wall (with an interior door) as both the essential building support and the partition dividing the main block in two parts. Both the support and rooms are aligned north-south.

The floors, originally earthen, were later covered by random-width timber held in place by hand-forged nails. The 22-foot-long shed-roof porch on the east, the attic and door under the eaves, and the single dormer in the roof of the south section on the east side appear to be nineteenth-century additions.

The five-room double cottage was a comfortable summer retreat for Rebecca and her children. Food and firewood were available. Produce grew in former gardens, and additional fruits and vegetables could be purchased from nearby farms. Rock Creek mills provided flour; there were fish in the streams; and berries, fruit, and nuts from bushes and trees supplemented the larder.

The cozy dwelling nestled in the trees and shrubs, surrounded by flowers, springs, and small animal life. There were large, lumbering yellow and black turtles, scampering rabbits, inquisitive squirrels, opossums, otter, chipmunks, and all species of birds and butterflies. There were Indian arrowheads and pottery shards to be found. The place was a natural playground for children.

It must have been an enchanted summer, reminiscent of Rebecca's childhood years at Sotterley. Most of all, Rebecca and her children were free of the stress of city living and the threat of impending war.

Fig. 4. *Rosedale, Southwest Corner and Facade*. (Photograph by Max Darrow, Youth for Understanding)

CHAPTER II

The Building of Rosedale
Forrest Additions, Interior and Exterior Furnishings

*A*s Rebecca wished, her husband added a wooden clapboard house on a foundation of stone to the modest summer cottage as a residence for their family. A rambling structure, it is composed of three rectangular sections connected to each other in front of and adjoining the two-part cottage in the rear. The joinings, imprecise and irregular, create a picturesque but architecturally imperfect dwelling.

The largest rectangle, approximately 53 by 15 feet, is positioned lengthwise, east-west, creating a wide southern facade for the center hall entrance. Across the front, Forrest added a ground-level verandah (later bricked), over which there was a shed roof supported by six slender wooden pillars with capitals and bases of simple design (fig. 4). This block, two storied and five bayed in front, with one bay and a modern grouping of three small bays on the second-story rear and no bays on the ground floor, is covered by a pitched roof and two tall brick end chimneys.

The second section, perhaps the first built, connects with the rear of the first section on the west side. A perpendicular appendage to the front, it runs north-south, the combination forming an L shape. Structurally similar to its companion, it is simpler architecturally with smaller dimensions. Its two chimneys are midway in a gently sloped roof. This portion is also two-storied, with a first-floor door and two bays on the east with three bays on the second floor, and three bays above and below on the west side. As Marion Lane's drawing shows (page iii), there was originally a shed-roof porch and probably a door on the west side, which were removed in the twentieth century.

Between the stone cottage and the two front frame units was added what may have been an afterthought, a third small, narrow wing, one and one-half stories with deeply sloped roof and dormer. This wing,

14   The Building of Rosedale

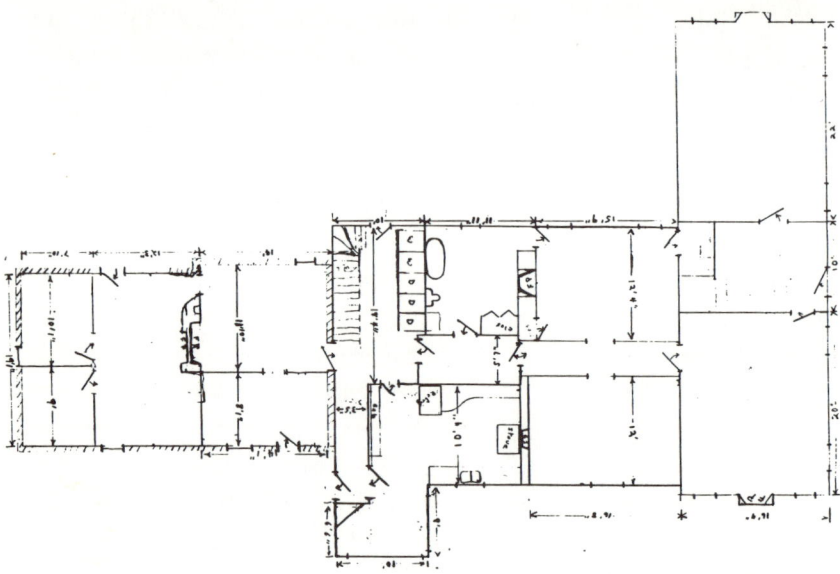

Fig. 5. *Rosedale, from above, West.* (Photograph by Max Darrow, Youth for Understanding); *Current Floor Plan.* (Courtesy Youth for Understanding)

which has been altered through the years, apparently was built to connect the old cottages with the new parts of the residence. It is 10 feet wide and protrudes from the western wall of the frame section 6 feet on one side and 9 on the other, with a separate entrance. On the east, the wing is flush with the frame block, but projects nearly 2 feet from the adjoining stone cottage wall. The view from above illustrates clearly the five sections of the house and the interplay of irregular roof levels, chimneys, and echoing wall shapes (fig. 5).

The stone cottages became the kitchen and servants' quarters. The narrow adjoining frame room could have served as a separation as well as a corridor between the working and the residential units of the Forrest home.

The exterior has changed little except for repairs and modifications, such as the removal of the west side porch. The entire house, including the stone cottages, is painted yellow, and the single color blends all disparate parts together harmoniously, rendering the residence eloquently visible, yet modestly integrated into the surrounding grounds and greenery.

The interior, although modified and modernized, appears to have retained much of its original floor plan. There is a large center entrance hall in which a half-turn stairway with landings begins at the back half of the hall's west wall. The plastered stair wall has an engaged handrail running its full length. The rail and balusters are plain and unadorned. Under the stairs there was originally a "lodging room."

On either side of the entrance hall is a spacious room with fireplace, one used as a drawing room or parlor, and the other for dining. At the rear of the room on the west, a door opens onto a long hall leading through the second frame section and into the wing and the original stone structures. This hall is flanked, dormitory fashion, by two rooms on either side.

The same floor plan is repeated on the second floor: a large bedroom on either side of a center hall, with a long hall from the west room that has two bedrooms on either side. Room sizes have been altered on both floors to accommodate baths and closets. Nearly every room in Forrest's additions has its own fireplace, differing in size, material, and trim but all simple and functional. The interior woodwork, including the fireplace trim, seems to be nineteenth or early twentieth century. It is believed that there was originally wood paneling on the lower half of the walls on the first floor. All that remains today is the sideboard of the stairs in the entrance hall, which is vertically paneled, and the dado of the west room, which is horizontally paneled.

Through the years there have been attempts to label Rosedale's architectural style. It has been described as a manor house, a colonial frame and stone, and a simple farmstead. Forrest family members have called the stone sections "the box" and the frame additions "an humble stretched-out barrack." Others have dismissed the structure as undistinguished.

For the architectural historian, however, Rosedale is an eighteenth-century gem. It is vernacular architecture in the truest sense, conforming to landscape and local customs, built with local materials, meeting the needs of the owner-builder, an example of growth rather than plan. It is also a running architectural narrative, which begins with the basic, English-inspired, eighteenth-century stone cottages, progresses to the more refined American frame additions, and culminates in the front rectangle, the face of which stylistically incorporates the symmetry and order characteristic of late eighteenth-century Federalist architecture. The placement of the entrance and porch make maximum use of the natural panorama, south, east, and west—an architectural mark of distinction in any period.

Perhaps the most fitting description of Rosedale's architecture is from the esteemed architect Frank Lloyd Wright, who commented on the honesty and appropriateness of the architectural style of the farmhouse. It is indeed an honest, unpretentious structure and, as such, has a unique dignity. It bespeaks the character and the way of life of the man who built it and the family who lived there.

Unique as the man responsible for its construction, Rosedale does not compare with the two neighboring estates built later—Woodley Oaks (ca. 1800) and the Highlands (1817-27). Rosedale predates them in time and purpose. These two masonry structures are *à la mode*, fashionable. For both houses plans were carefully drawn and followed;

skilled craftsmen were employed. They represent the so-called polite and self-conscious nineteenth-century architecture. If Rosedale must be labeled, it might be called eighteenth-century Forrest functionalism!

The Forrest home, at first glance, resembles and was undoubtedly influenced by Sotterley, the Plater plantation on the Patuxent that was Rebecca's family home. The placement, the view, the facade with its elongated and columned porch, and the fact that Sotterley, too, was built in sections, are the same (fig. 6). Sotterley was, however, well planned. It was begun by the original owner, James Bowles, ca. 1711. After 1729 the structure was slowly enlarged by several generations of the Plater family. Pattern books and talented workmen were used. Sixty to one hundred servants were available to assist. The interior wood trim is a work of art. Building materials were imported when necessary.

Rosedale, on the other hand, is Forrest-built with local labor, materials, and in a short time. Uriah Forrest had little leisure to build an impressive, elegant, personal abode, for he was an overextended professional man with a growing family. He had, at most, five servants to assist him, supplemented by nearby planters who served as workmen when they were available. Haste and limited help could account for the variation in shape and size of the different units and the unstudied informality of the whole.

Subsequent Forrest-built houses in Georgetown and the Federal City demonstrate knowledge and skill in construction. Those houses are brick, stately, and well balanced, built according to the fashion of the day and the plans found in builder's handbooks.

By all accounts, Rebecca Forrest, mistress of Rosedale, was a woman of modest and unassuming tastes. She is recalled as being proud but lacking in vanity, one who preferred her garden to her house and her family's welfare over social status. The exterior mode and the interior furnishings of Rosedale are in keeping with this appraisal of its mistress's personality. Rebecca's furniture was adequate, practical, and well made, inviting but not luxurious. Her china, silver, glassware, and table linens were elaborate, however, appropriate to serve Forrest's illustrious friends.

Fig. 6. *Sotterley Mansion*, ca. 1711. Plater family home, St. Mary's County, Maryland. Pencil sketch by John Moll, Oxford, Maryland. (Permission of the artist)

The Building of Rosedale

Among Rebecca's most precious possessions were imports from Europe and the Orient, some of which were undoubtedly acquired by Uriah Forrest during his years as an overseas shipping merchant. Some were family heirlooms. Others were custom made for the farm.

Fireplaces provided warmth for the rooms; those in the kitchen served for cooking as well. There were candles for light in freestanding silver candelabra, in table-size silver candlesticks, and, for daily service, small candle holders of pewter or iron with glass chimneys.

The kitchen equipment was practical, geared to open fireplace cooking. There were iron pots, frying pans, a griddle, drip pan, spits, a "Bell" metal skillet, copper kettles, and milk pans. For more epicurean culinary needs, there were dutch ovens, molds, spice mills, and a marble mortar. Kitchenware was pewter; fireplace fixtures were iron.

For sewing done in the home, there was a supply of needles, thimbles, and scissors; four spinning wheels to make yarn and thread; and four smoothing irons for pressing.

The Forrests furnished the sizable dining room to accommodate the numerous guests frequently served at Rosedale. Uriah Forrest was in his prime and enjoying his successes—his position, his property, his wealth, his family, and his friends. He was an amiable man, wise and well liked. At Rosedale, Forrest was host to presidents, cabinet members, congressmen, District Commissioners, to men of high or low degree. Using his assets and influence, he was a patron to those in need and frequently helped with their problems. Men who came to discuss business, politics, and war usually stayed for dinner and often overnight, for evening travel on the narrow, rutted, and unlighted roads was difficult.

Rebecca had been trained from childhood in the social amenities. Devoted to her husband, she was a gracious hostess, setting a splendid table and serving excellent meals. Meals at that time were a gastronomical extravaganza with innumerable courses and choices. A rich display of food was equated with the affluence of the host. Beef and veal were preferred. Seafood, terrapin, fowl, and game were often included, usually with sauces or heavily marinated with the favorite colonial wine, Madeira. Vegetables were creamed; bread and pastries

Fig. 9. *Dining Table*. Mahogany, Hepplewhite design, sectional, can be extended to more than eleven feet. Believed to be the table that came to Rosedale from the Forrest house in Georgetown and the one around which the president, commissioners, and proprietors dined and negotiated for land for the Federal City, March 29, 1791. Note bell tower of National Cathedral in distance. (Faulkner Family Collection)

room when needed. In it were one dozen green Windsor chairs, a walnut clothes hanger, and a small dining table.

The drawing room was curtained, carpeted, and contained a calico-covered sofa and pillows, arm and side chairs (leather bottomed), an English drop-leaf breakfast table, a tea table, a mahogany card table, an "elegant French clock" (a gift from Pierre L'Enfant), marble China ornaments, and a King George tobacco box, large enough for a pipe (figs. 10, 11, 12). The ample fireplace, possibly an original, is brick with black slate and a simple classical mantel and trim.

There were pictures on the walls. Two of special interest were samplers in floral design embroidered on silk cloth by Elizabeth, the Forrests' eldest daughter. The landscape medallions in the center are worked with the hair of her parents and siblings, an ancient custom (fig. 13). End tables and silver candlesticks completed the furnishing.

Uriah Forrest did much work at home and kept a well-equipped office. As the accompanying illustration shows (fig. 14), his desk was impressive—a lustrous light mahogany secretaire bookcase desk with flat top, diamond and arched astragals, fitted drawers, with a cupboard with additional drawers below and a shaped apron with bracket feet. He also had work tables, stools, sets of wooden pigeon holes (vertical files) on a wooden table, writing materials, and a set of paper weights. There were custom-made bookcases for his extensive collection of reading matter. On the shelves were three volumes of *The Laws of the States*, a copy of Harris's *Entries*, Kilty's *Laws of Maryland*, and other significant legal editions. The overflow from the bookcases was stored in leather trunks.

Bedroom floors were carpeted, and beds and windows were curtained for privacy and warmth. Bedsteads were mahogany, pine, or walnut, as were the bureaus and tables. There were small beds for the children and larger beds for the adults. A miniature porcelain tea set and a small lead rooster numbered among the toys in the children's rooms. Mirrors were freestanding "dressing glasses," some Japanese, others domestic. Drinking water was provided in water bottles with tumblers on end tables.

The most thoughtfully furnished room, "upstairs above the dining

Fig. 10. *English Drop-Leaf Breakfast Table.* Eighteenth century, 36 by 13 1/2 inches. Mahogany with curved leaves, rope-turned legs, and a single end drawer. (Forrest-Rosedale Collection; photograph by Henry Leonhardt)

Fig. 11. *French Clock.* Eighteenth century, oblong ebony base, trimmed in gilt and enamel. The clock is supported by two slender figurine columns with pointed crown above. The pendulum is free swinging; the numerals are arabic. A gift to Uriah Forrest from Pierre Charles L'Enfant, it was originally covered by a glass dome. The clock was advertised for auction at Rosedale in 1802, but is still in the possession of the Forrest family. (Forrest-Rosedale Collection)

The Building of Rosedale

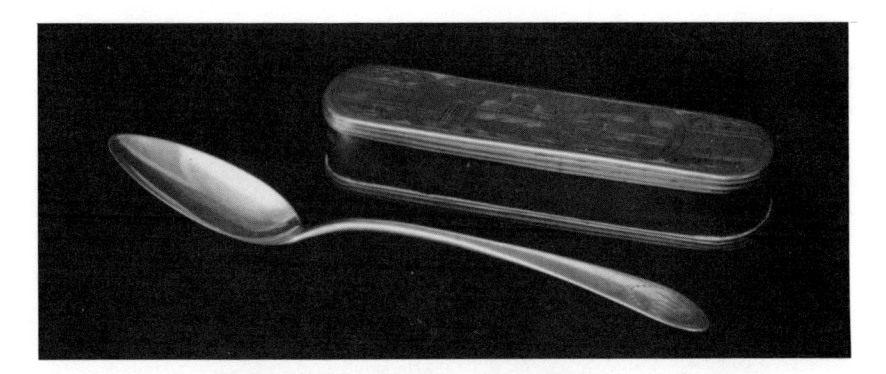

Fig. 12. *Tobacco Box and Silver Spoon.* The eighteenth-century tobacco box, 6 1/4 by 1 1/4 inches, was traditionally made of polished horn or wood with a silver base and brass lid engraved with a genre landscape. It is small enough to carry in a pocket and large enough to hold a pipe. Eighteenth century silver spoon is marked "Bright cut, George III, London, 1787". Forrest's silver is plain except for a raised dot oval crest encircling a calligraphic initial "F". (Forrest-Rosedale Collection; photograph by Henry Leonhardt)

Fig. 13. *Side Chairs and Silk Samplers.* Hepplewhite-style mahogany side chairs, hand carved at Sotterley Plantation for the Forrests, ca. 1789. Pierced shield backs carved with husks and paterae with tapered legs. The framed silk samplers, 15 by 18 inches, were embroidered by Elizabeth, eldest child of Rebecca and Uriah Forrest. (Forrest-Rosedale Collection; photograph by Henry Leonhardt)

Fig. 14. *Uriah Forrest's Desk*. Eighteenth century, Mahogany. (Forrest-Rosedale Collection; photograph by Henry Leonhardt)

The Building of Rosedale 27

Fig. 15. *Rebecca's Bible with Silver Goblet.* The Bible is personal size, 4 1/2 by 7 inches, maroon leather, embossed in gold. The center design on the cover is a floral motif framing the name, "Rebecca Plater". The well-worn Bible retains a clear image of Rebecca's beautiful script and the records of her children's births and christenings. The silver goblet is the same style as the spoon, with the Forrest crest the only decoration. (Forrest-Rosedale Collection; photograph by Henry Leonhardt)

room" in the southeast corner of the front section, appears to have been the master bedroom. On the floor was a canvas cover cloth topped by a large Wilton carpet (English wool with design) and a small matching Wilton for the bedside. The room included two curtained bedsteads (one mahogany, one pine), a pine dressing table, a washstand with bowl and pitcher, a pyramid table with glasses and decanter, a plate warmer, and Rebecca's maroon leather Bible (fig. 15).

The linen supply, consisting of sheets, blankets, coverlets, pillows, and pillowcases, was adequate for the family, the help, and guests. Special coverings worthy of mention were the white counterpanes (stitched quilts) and a quilt of "unusual design" imported from Marseilles.

Rosedale was more than a country residence with a hospitable table where notables gathered; it was a self-sufficient working farm. The farmstead that provided most of the household needs was the life-style to which Rebecca and Uriah Forrest were accustomed; it was part of their Southern Maryland heritage, transported to the area of the Federal City. Forrest, a planter's son, grew lush fields of grain and planted extensive gardens where vegetables and fruits thrived. His asparagus beds were so successful he was able to share the roots with neighbors and friends so they could grow their own. The grape arbors produced "delicious" fruit, as did his fig trees and berry bushes.

Granddaughter Maria notes that Rebecca's "delight was in her garden . . . her happiness in . . . horticulture." In a small garden near the house Rebecca planted the customary herbs for medicine, spices, and tea. Compactly arranged, the herb garden had stepping-stone paths; one of the stones, a blue granite hand-turned millstone (a quern) quarried from nearby Broad Branch, may be seen on the property today (fig. 16).

It is said that artist and friend Pierre L'Enfant was Rebecca's landscape adviser. The vista in front of the residence was enhanced by terracing the hilly terrain; on the terraces were multiple rows of fruit trees and flowers. Terraces became avenues. On the west side, there was

The Building of Rosedale

Fig. 16. *Quern Stepping Stone*. Early eighteenth century. The blue granite millstone may be seen in the brick pathway on the west side of Rosedale's entrance. (Photograph by author)

Fig. 17. *Original Terrace, Rosedale*. A portion of an eighteenth-century terrace on the grounds in front of the Rosedale residence. Made of local stone. Located today off the path from the Newark Street gate. (Photograph by author)

Peach Walk and Pear Walk; on the east, Cherry Walk and Apple Walk (fig. 17). A greenhouse on the east separated the vegetable garden from the orchard. A spring in the valley in front and another "halfway up the orchard" added to the picture.

Rebecca's gardens in the spring and summer were a celebration of color. Blossoming fruit trees, redbud, dogwood, laurel, and wild and cultivated flowers along tidy walks and meandering springs could have only been a joy to behold, a breathtaking addition to what was naturally a beautiful view.

The accessory buildings fanned out in the rear. These consisted of a large barn for the livestock, a dairy, a granary, a cornhouse, poultry house, and smokehouse. There were "commodious stables," a carriage house, and, beyond, small houses for workmen.

An inventory of tools reflects the self-contained nature of farming and carpentry at Rosedale: lumber, crowbars, grindstones, saws, weeding and grubbing hoes, "madicks," spades, shovels, rakes, "ploughs," harrows, and pitchforks. In the stables were "two valuable carriage horses," a small bay, several other equines, and mules.

The family carriages, including Uriah Forrest's silver-trimmed vehicle with silver harness crafted especially for him in Annapolis, were sheltered in the carriage house. The silver inlaid carriage was Forrest's most important possession, for it was his mobility. He was uncomfortable on horseback and could walk only with crutches. The carriage had become the courageous amputee's cachet.

CHAPTER III

Landholder, Bankrupt, Clerk of Court
Rosedale Saved

With his family happily ensconced at Rosedale, the owner-builder turned his attention to his business and governmental responsibilities. Uriah Forrest, a man who inherited neither wealth nor position, was now one of the largest landholders in and around the Federal City, an incorporator and board member of the newly organized Bank of Columbia and the Georgetown Bridge Company authorized by the Maryland legislature to implement the growth of the city, and a representative from Maryland to the Third Congress of the United States. In addition, he was soon to be appointed brigadier general in the militia—the American substitute for a standing army.

Forrest's property acquisitions were consistent with the Anglo-American tradition that land was money. Convinced that the value of acreage in the area of the Federal City would escalate as the capital city developed, Forrest invested most of the fortune he had gained as a postwar consignment merchant in local land. In addition to his partial ownership of Pretty Prospects on a portion of which he built Rosedale, he owned outright hundreds of acres in upper Montgomery County, approximately 2,000 more in partnership with Benjamin Stoddert, at least 150 lots in the Federal City, and houses and lots in Georgetown. Forrest also patented more than 1,000 acres in Allegany County and 243.5 acres in St. Mary's County, and he owned a house and lot in Alexandria, Virginia.

Forrest and Benjamin Stoddert dissolved their lucrative shipping partnership by mutual consent in 1793, and Uriah Forrest directed his business acumen to the management of his properties and the support of the Federal City project. As a precaution, he kept a partial interest in several sailing vessels.

A welcome addition to his material wealth was Forrest's wealth of family and friends. By 1799, Rebecca and Uriah were parents of five children: Elizabeth, August 6, 1791; Benjamin Stoddert, October 22, 1792; George Plater, July 14, 1794; Ann, January 12, 1797; and Maria, March 3, 1799.

With parents deceased, Rebecca's brother, George IV, and Uriah's brother, Zachariah, as eldest sons, inherited the bulk of their families' holdings and were content to remain in St. Mary's County. George IV stayed at Sotterley, struggling to maintain the estate in the tradition of his ancestors. He relied on Uriah for advice and assistance and in return supervised Forrest's plantation at Half Pone Point near Sotterley. Zachariah Forrest was appointed a justice and commissioner of tax in St. Mary's and was comfortably settled there.

Other family members on both sides followed Uriah's pattern and migrated to the area of the Federal City. Younger brother Zephaniah Forrest bought land in Montgomery County's Fifth District in 1793. Zachariah's two sons, Joseph and Richard, left St. Mary's for upper Montgomery County, where Joseph became a landowner in 1798.

Richard Forrest, a favorite nephew, had been employed by Forrest & Stoddert to go to England to supervise what was left of the partners' shipping business. He stayed in London until he was notified that as a result of international tension, the commission business was a "total failure." Richard was ultimately appointed fourth postmaster of Georgetown from 1796 to 1798. He lived in Georgetown near his good friends Dr. and Mrs. William Thornton, all of whom were frequent visitors to Rosedale.

Thomas and John Plater, Rebecca's brothers, were also in town and located on Forrest property. Thomas, who owned one of the Forrest-built double houses in Georgetown, married Ann Lingan, sister of the General's close friend James Lingan. John, who bought a lot in a Forrest-owned Georgetown block, later built a fine country home on Pretty Prospects land near the intersection of today's Woodley Road and Wisconsin Avenue, which he named Greenwood. Nephew Henry Forrest bought 50 acres of Pretty Prospects near Connecticut Avenue, where he built his home, Redwood. Neither Plater-built house is extant.

The final *émigrés* were Rebecca's sister Elizabeth and her husband Philip Barton Key (uncle of Francis Scott Key, author of "The Star-Spangled Banner"). Key, an attorney and former chief justice of the Fourth United States Circuit Court, moved to Georgetown, where he established a private practice. He later bought 250 acres of Forrest's land near Rosedale, on which he built his neoclassical mansion, Woodley Oaks, now known as Woodley.

Thus, Uriah Forrest became the patriarch of a large brood. There seems to have been a warm relationship among the Forrests, their brothers, sisters, and nephews. Rebecca's brothers called her Becky, and Uriah was respectfully known as the General.

In addition to family, the gregarious general had an ever-widening circle of friends whom he entertained at Rosedale. Forrest's reputation for loyalty had become a legend in the Federal City, perhaps because he had dared befriend Pierre L'Enfant in his dispute with the District Commissioners and had attempted to play peacemaker when L'Enfant's replacement, surveyor Andrew Ellicott, found himself in a similar situation. President Washington had been forced to dismiss the excitable French artist-engineer as city planner in 1792 because of his conflict with the commissioners. Andrew Ellicott, facing the same dissension L'Enfant had encountered, angrily resigned his position shortly after his appointment in spite of Forrest's pleas for conciliation.

Forrest was also a friend and confidant to George Washington. They had much in common. They were both Tidewater men; Forrest had served under General Washington's command in the Revolutionary War; and, politically, they were staunch Federalists. George Washington's respect for Uriah Forrest in business and politics is seen throughout the president's correspondence. On at least two occasions he recommended Forrest for important government positions.

It is often said that as president, Washington dined at Rosedale, but there are no reliable sources to verify this assertion. It is possible that the president dined at Forrest's country home as he had dined at Forrest's home in Georgetown, for the two men were deeply involved in the Federal City project and had frequent discussions about its problems. George Washington is known to have preferred business dinners over social ones.

Forrest was a personal friend of the second president of the United States, John Adams, for whom he gave a large dinner party at Rosedale on a warm Friday afternoon on June 6, 1800, to which local denizens and other prominent men were invited. A crusty and somewhat antisocial New Englander, the president left the gathering early as was his custom, Mrs. William Thornton later reported in her diary.

Although there is no documentation of a friendship between Forrest and former Vice-President Aaron Burr, Isabel Green Zantzinger, Uriah's great-great-granddaughter, writes that Burr sought the general's counsel and guidance following his disastrous duel with his political enemy Alexander Hamilton. Burr killed Hamilton in the duel and, because of it, had become an outcast. Mrs. Zantzinger states that although Uriah Forrest "condemned" Burr's action, he sympathized with the sorrowing man and permitted him to visit Rosedale. There Burr spent "three weeks wandering over hills and woods" until he regained his composure.

Even with his infirmity, the pain of which increased in his middle years, Uriah Forrest continued to travel, making his way on crutches and riding in his silver-trimmed carriage. He went to St. Mary's to help his brother-in-law settle Sotterley debts and to confer with kinsman William Peregrine Fitzhugh on political matters. He made frequent trips to Georgetown and the Federal City for business, political, and social dinners. He dined in the port city with Tobias Lear, President Washington's secretary, and with Notley Young, John Mason, and others. He joined financier Robert Morris and Englishman Thomas Law (who married Martha Washington's granddaughter) for dinner at the Union Tavern in Georgetown. He met city leaders at the home of Dr. and Mrs. William Thornton, even on cold snowy winter evenings, to arrange funding for the Federal City.

Forrest must have especially enjoyed his old-guard Federalist cronies who assembled regularly at the home of Thomas Sim Lee, former general in the Revolutionary War and former governor of Maryland. When Lee retired from public service, he built a home on the north corner of today's 30th and M streets in Georgetown, where he wintered, gathering political and social friends about him. There, it is said, war stories were recounted and politics debated. The Lee home is extant, presently serving as a business establishment.

It was Lee who, as governor of Maryland, appointed Uriah Forrest general during the crisis of 1794. When the war between Great Britain and France threatened to draw America into the maelstrom, the president called out fifteen hundred militiamen from four states. Governor Lee rallied the Maryland quota and appointed officers, one of whom was Uriah Forrest, commissioned brigadier general for Montgomery County in the state of Maryland.

Forrest had been compelled to retire as a colonel in the Continental forces in 1781 by his battle-induced amputation; with this appointment thirteen years later, his military career came full circle. He bore his new title with pride. It was one by which he was known the remainder of his life.

Fortunately the General was not called upon to lead men into battle again. With the help of the infant United States and its emissary John Jay, the French and English agreed to negotiate a treaty of friendship, and the friction abated between the mighty powers.

General Uriah Forrest's relatively peaceful interlude of prosperity and prominence began to deteriorate by 1797, the result of a general economic crisis in the United States and the collapse of the Morris-Nicholson syndicate in the Federal City, the epicenter of the quaking American economy.

Financing the Federal City was a problem from the inception of the project. The Residence Bill did not provide sufficient funding for an undertaking as monumental as building a capital city. It mandated the president to select a site, appoint commissioners, accept grants of land or money, and, with congressional approval, to borrow. Maryland and Virginia advanced a total of $192,000; Uriah Forrest and other proprietors donated land to the government for streets, avenues, and public squares and sold, at a reduced price, the land needed for public buildings and grounds. The remaining land, laid out in lots, was divided equally between the proprietors and the city. It was a generous agreement on the part of the proprietors and would have benefited both parties had the economy been stable and the lot sales profitable.

The economy of the new republic was weak; and Federal City lot sales were a dismal disappointment. In an attempt to encourage investors, the president and the District Commissioners permitted a syndicate composed of Robert Morris, John Nicholson, and James Greenleaf to buy approximately seven thousand city lots from the project directors and proprietors—with little money down and on a promise-to-pay-when-sold basis.

The syndicate's failure had a domino effect in the city. The insolvent group could not pay either the commissioners or a proprietor like Forrest for the lots it had bought on credit. Forrest, who bought his lots on the same terms as Morris-Nicholson, was therefore also unable to pay the commissioners. In the meantime, Forrest, several other proprietors, and the commissioners had pledged their personal holdings to the state of Maryland to secure loans to bolster the city's economy. The Maryland loans were due, and there was no money to pay them.

Forrest's extensive landholdings now became a liability. He had no cash flow, and when the market collapsed, property was almost worthless and sales at a standstill. Many investors in the Federal City became insolvent or were petitioned into bankruptcy.

General Forrest could not forestall insolvency, but, with the help of brother-in-law Philip Barton Key, he salvaged his home. Key, who had escaped financial reverses and was indebted to Uriah Forrest for past favors, accepted a mortgage on Rosedale and title to certain personal property but granted Forrest lifetime use of them.

Uriah Forrest sold what property he could. Friends such as James Lingan, Dr. Ninian McGruder, and Daniel Reintzell, former mayor of Georgetown, bought small parcels of land from Forrest, but there still was not money enough to cover what was owed. By August 1802, Forrest was sued for debts totaling more than $23,000, and he was petitioned into bankruptcy under the first Bankruptcy Act of the United States, an involuntary proceeding passed by the Congress in 1800. His two major creditors were the District Commissioners and the state of Maryland.

On November 16, 1802, the *National Intelligencer and Washington Advertiser* announced a marshal's sale of the remainder of Forrest's personal and real property at Barney's Tavern and the Rosedale estate. The land was to be auctioned at the tavern in the morning, and the personal property at Rosedale, "The Dwelling House of General Forrest, about a mile and a half above Georgetown," in the late afternoon.

The scene at Rosedale must have been as bleak as the month in which the sale was held. Rebecca's beautiful gardens were barren and brown. There was a chill in the air as the sun sank in the western sky, casting oblique shadows on the house and grounds where family belongings were spread out for all to see.

The General, on crutches, moved among the assembled—bona fide purchasers as well as the curious, the gloating, and the greedy. There were items in the auction that he could not bear to lose, and some he knew would be needed. Forrest reclaimed five sheep, two cows, one pig, six Windsor chairs, a walnut and a mahogany chest, carpentry and garden tools, his favorite "cloathes" press and plate warmer, "kitching furniture and Sundries." He bought these on credit, for he had no cash. The total of his purchases amounted to $247, which was paid after his death in the probate settlement, with interest added of $58.67.

Many good men suffered severe financial reverses in the crash of 1797. Among them were Benjamin Stoddert, Thomas Sim Lee, Francis and Charles Lowndes, John Threlkeld, Thomas Addison, and Thomas Law. Given the circumstances, Uriah Forrest fared better than most, if not with finances certainly with dignity. While fellow insolvents responded to their fate with anger, despair, humiliation, mental and physical ill health, Forrest maintained an equanimity, inventoried his assets, retained what he could, and kept his sanity and an adequate lifestyle the rest of his days.

The suits by the state of Maryland and the District Commissioners were settled for court costs as a result of a decision by the Jefferson administration that the Treasury of the United States was responsible for payment of the Maryland loans. This action released the 420 acres of Rosedale land that Forrest had mortgaged to Maryland as partial security for a loan to save the Federal City. Other cases were settled with promises to pay the principal in installments.

Forrest's family, his farm, and a position as the first clerk of the newly formed United States Circuit Court of the District of Columbia were the impetus for survival. When President John Adams was defeated by Democratic-Republican Thomas Jefferson in 1800, Adams angrily appointed a legion of faithful Federalists, many of whom had lost their wealth attempting to found the Federal City, to judicial positions. Among the so-called midnight judges appointed was "The Honorable Uriah Forrest as Justice of the Peace for the County of Washington in the District of Columbia." On the orders of President Jefferson, the new secretary of state, James Madison, did not deliver the commissions, thereby rendering them ineffective. This episode precipitated the famous Supreme Court case of *Marbury* v. *Madison*, which was filed by William Marbury, Dennis Ramsay, Robert Townsend Hooe, and William Harper, who had also lost appointments as justices of the peace. Fortuitously, the Jeffersonian purge left the circuit court untouched, and the sympathetic judges appointed Adams's old friend Uriah Forrest as their first clerk.

With neither a state nor a municipal court in Washington, the Circuit Court of the District of Columbia was an all-encompassing arm of the judiciary, and its clerk, a responsible legal officer. The hourly wage of the clerk was equivalent to the attorney general's—$5 per hour, plus additional fees for special services. It was a modest salary when compared with Forrest's remuneration as auditor of the state of Maryland more than a decade before in St. Mary's County.

As there was no building for the circuit court, it shared a room adjoining the Senate Chamber with the Supreme Court. The office of the clerk was moved from time to time to whatever space was available,

Landholder, Bankrupt, Clerk of Court

and Forrest was permitted to work at Rosedale when the court was not in session. As an officer of the court, he was also permitted to perform services at home for fees.

The General increased the equipment in his Rosedale office. Using J. March as his supplier, he ordered—through May 1805—approximately five hundred quills for writing, reams of foolscap (legal paper), black sand and pounce (a fine powder used to size porous surfaces of paper or parchment), blotting paper, Indian Rubber (erasers), bound folio books, and reams of folio paper "wove thin." A. and G. Way printed two quires each of marriage licenses and writs for his use.

It was good to work at home. Forrest, with his multiple endeavors, had been a traveler for many years. Seated at his splendid mahogany desk on his own comfortable chair, surrounded by book-laden shelves and legal treatises, worktables, files, paper, pens, and legal forms, the general had a complete office, adequate for private practice and unfinished court chores.

Through the open window he could see the rolling hills and terraces of Rosedale, the planted fields, the stately trees. He could breathe the clean air, hear his children at play, and smell the pungent odors from the kitchen. He could watch the seasons change, the new buds of spring, the colorful flowers of summer, and the tumbling leaves of fall. He could see the quiet snows of winter as they brushed against the hand-blown leaded glass panes that reflected the flickering fireplace inside.

For Uriah Forrest this was a time of renewal, a time to tend to Rosedale and those things long neglected during the pressure of his careers and his bankruptcy. In a flurry of credit spending, the General took command of the farm. He began by repairing Rosedale's tools. Michael Brady, a local handyman, was hired to sharpen rakes, "coutters and mattocks," to replace hardware, and to mend "tugg chains." Horses were groomed and shod.

Livestock barriers of thornbushes and wooden fences were replaced. From Isaac Pierce, a Rock Creek neighbor, and Thomas Main, nearly seven hundred thornbushes were purchased and planted. Sixty-five panels of post-and-rail and two new gates were installed by Thomas

Spriggs Belt, another neighbor.

Orchards were replenished with young fruit trees, and new grass was sown in between. Isaac Pierce hauled hay, barley, flaxseed, and other grains to the farm. Loads of manure from William Duvall were spread to energize the earth.

The house was painted and plastered. The General's silver-trimmed carriage was renovated, its spoke plates replaced. The larder was stocked. What was not grown at Rosedale was purchased. Adam King and Co., Georgetown, delivered wines, sherry, porter (a dark beer), Madeira, whiskey, coffee, sugar, fine flour, cheese, peas, and raisins. Fruit was ordered pending the improvement of the orchard yield. Two extra full-time hands were hired—a couple, Bromwell and Ruth Welsh, who were "free men." They were paid $8 per month.

Rebecca bought new silver spoons from Riggs of Georgetown. She arranged tutoring for the children. A Forrest daughter was enrolled at Mrs. Smith's boarding school, where she received dancing instructions from "Monsieur Generes."

The General polished his personal appearance. He had regular "shavings and combings" from James Gannon at Rosedale and at Gannon's shop in the city. He ordered new gold links for his shirts, "eyes for buttons," and sent his watch for repair to Charles Burnett in Georgetown.

CHAPTER IV

Uriah Forrest's Final Years

Action had always sustained him, but the once-indefatigable General was tiring. The stresses of time and extended activity were undermining his strength. Uriah Forrest was suffering from asthma as well as the chronic pain in his amputated limb, where the open flap surgical technique had prevented healing. On his trips home from town these days, he stopped his carriage at Rosedale's Georgetown to Frederick Road entrance and waited patiently for someone to open the gate for him—a task he had formerly done for himself.

Rebecca was in charge of household health and home remedies. She had been well trained at Sotterley, where the mistress and her daughters were expected to care for the family and staff. Rebecca's first aid and temporary medical assistance were supplemented by the ofttimes more than weekly visits of their physician, Dr. Charles Worthington of Georgetown. Home visits were customary; office visits were rare; and apothecaries, nonexistent. Doctors traveled from house to house, bringing medications and the tools of their trade with them, mixing and treating on site.

Dr. Worthington visited Rosedale for years, dispensing cathartics, astringent powders, antimum (antimony powder, medicinal salts of metallic origin), camphoral mint, and saline juleps. He treated not only the Forrests but their extended household, as was the custom. In the six months between June and December 1802, Dr. Worthington made at least twenty-five house calls to Rosedale, tending the needs of "Carpenter Harry," Aaron, "a negro man," a "negro girl," Mrs. Forrest, the General, and eight-year-old "Master George Forrest."

He regularly prescribed "Pectoral Juleps" for the General's asthma and soothing antiseptics for his amputated leg. Cathartics were the medication most often prescribed for the family and staff. To supplement the medication, quantities of Syder (cider), a well-known rural remedy for constipation, were ordered from a local merchant.

The doctor became a friend as well as a physician to General Forrest. They were of the same vintage. Doctor Worthington was a member of the old school, dignified and serious. Born in Anne Arundel County in Southern Maryland, he, too, had migrated to Georgetown, where he established a large and responsible practice and became the first president of the District of Columbia Medical Society.

He was described as: "An austere man . . . he dressed in the old style; his hair in queue, knee britches, long stockings, and buckles on his shoes." Dr. Worthington drove a coach-and-four when going to his country place near Brightwood. He was a member of the vestry of St. John's Episcopal Church in Georgetown. A kindly man, he treated the Forrests even when they were unable to pay.

Forrest's health continued to deteriorate. Perhaps with a premonition of impending death, he wrote his own lengthy and explicit will on June 22, 1805 (fig. 18). Charles Worthington, John Threlkeld, former Georgetown mayor, and Forrest's nephew Joseph were summoned to Rosedale as witnesses. They reported him in good spirits and of sound and clear mind.

On July 3, 1805, Dr. Worthington made his last visit to Rosedale to treat his friend the General. The diagnosis, "Vitriol Infection"; the charge, $1. Three days later, Uriah Forrest died on the calico couch in the parlor of his beloved Rosedale. It was Saturday, July 6, 1805, in the twenty-ninth year after the signing of the Declaration of Independence. As could be expected, Uriah Forrest had continued to work to the end of his days. His final publication as clerk of the court appeared in the *National Intelligencer and Washington Advertiser*, Monday, July 8, 1805, two days after his death. It was a bankruptcy notice, the case of one John Frost, an insolvent debtor.

Devastated by her loss, Rebecca had little time to grieve, for death was a family affair and there was much to do. In the absence of undertakers, bodies of the deceased were laid out at home in simple shrouds. Family and friends were notified, and funeral arrangements made.

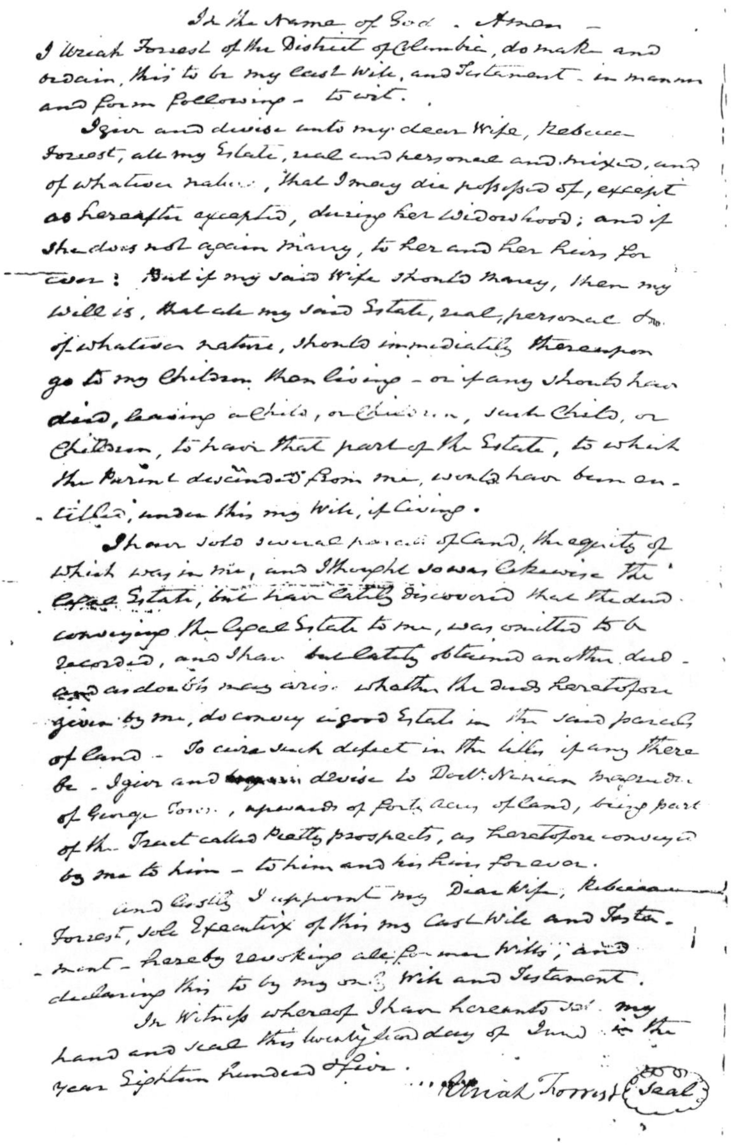

In the Name of God . Amen –

I Uriah Forrest of the District of Columbia, do make and ordain, this to be my last Will, and Testament – in manner and form following – to wit.

I give and devise unto my dear Wife, Rebecca Forrest, all my Estate, real and personal and mixed, and of whatever nature, that I may die possessed of, except as hereafter excepted, during her Widowhood; and if she does not again marry, to her and her heirs for ever: But if my said Wife should marry, then my will is, that all my said Estate, real, personal &c. of whatever nature, should immediately thereupon go to my Children then living – or if any should have died, leaving a Child, or Children, such Child, or Children, to have that part of the Estate, to which the Parent descended from me, would have been entitled, under this my Will, if living.

I have sold several parcels of Land, the equity of which was in me, and I thought so was likewise the legal Estate, but have lately discovered that the deed conveying the legal Estate to me, was omitted to be recorded, and I have but lately obtained another deed – and as doubts may arise whether the deeds heretofore given by me, do convey a good Estate in the said parcels of land – To cure such defect in the titles if any there be – I give and devise to Doct. Ninian Magruder of George Town, upwards of forty acres of land, being part of the Tract called Pretty prospects, as heretofore conveyed by me to him – to him and his heirs forever.

And lastly I appoint my Dear Wife, Rebecca Forrest, sole Executrix of this my last Will and Testament – hereby revoking all former Wills; and declaring this to be my only Will and Testament.

In Witness whereof I have hereunto set my hand and seal this twenty second day of June in the year Eighteen hundred & five. ... Uriah Forrest (Seal)

Fig. 18. *Portion of Uriah Forrest's Will.*

The Forrests owned a family plot (lot 275), at the Presbyterian Burial Ground at the southeast corner of what is today 30th and M streets in Georgetown. A section of the plot was prepared, and the grave dug. A coffin was readied by William King, a merchant in Virginia. Caskets were customarily simple, sometimes hexagonal in shape, made of pine, handcrafted by local cabinetmakers. General Forrest's casket was covered with black cloth, lined and trimmed ("plinced"). A hearse was ordered with horses and livery.

The interior of Rosedale was draped with yards of black cambric muslin, which framed the casket in funerary fashion. A black crepe was mounted on the entrance door of the residence. Mourning garments were assembled of black cashmere, silk, and ribbon.

Friends and family came to the farm to pay their respects. The day of the funeral a black velvet pall was draped over the coffin when it was moved from the house to the waiting hearse. There followed a solemn procession that wound through the flowered fields of Rosedale accompanied by the sound of clopping hooves, creaking carriage wheels, singing birds, and humming insects.

The hearse stopped at the gate, which was opened for the last time for General Forrest. Passing through, in quiet parade, came the hearse and mourners, the family and friends in carriages and on horseback. Turning left on the Frederick Road toward Georgetown, the funeral cortege traveled slowly down the hill on rutted roads to High Street, and thence to the burying yard beside Mr. Balch's Presbyterian meetinghouse.

Pallbearers wore black gloves with black crepes on their hats, adornments often worn by dignitaries for a month or more after the internment of the deceased. The family was dressed in black with black gloves. The widow's gloves and scarf were black silk.

Details of the service are not recorded, but by Presbyterian custom, it would have been a solemn affair. The Reverend Thomas Bloomer Balch would have led prayers and eulogies, either at the graveside or the following Sunday in church. When the casket was finally lowered into the grave, the sexton tolled the meetinghouse bells to signal the loss of the leader of the Forrest clan—a patriot, an outstanding citizen, a war hero, a battle casualty, a noteworthy legislator, a founding father of the Federal City, and a descendant of the founders of his country.

The obituary in the *Maryland Gazette* described Uriah Forrest well: "He embarked in early life in the Revolutionary War and served with distinction until the Battle of Germantown. Fated ever after to support himself on crutches and to be a prey to the evils of impaired health, his active and intelligent mind rose superior to misfortune and his life had been equally distinguished by honorable and useful enterprise."

In later years General Forrest was paid the following perceptive tribute: "He was happy in penetrating into the secret designs of others never disclosing more of his own inclinations than was necessary for the purpose at hand. His carriage was generally uniform and unaffectedly affable, his conversation enlivened by his vivacity; his knowledge and understanding strikingly quick and his talents to gain popularity were almost absolute. He possessed great penetration and discernment, with a sagacity not easily improved upon with an industry and vigilance indefatigable, rather an easy debater with a great command of his passions and affections, raising him superior to more improved minds."

Fig. 19. *Rebecca Forrest in Maturity*. Oil on canvas by Madame B. May. (Forrest-Rosedale Collection)

CHAPTER V

Rosedale After Forrest

The demise of General Uriah Forrest nearly sounded the death knell for his family home, Rosedale. His grief-stricken widow, as executrix of his estate, was overwhelmed by her husband's debts and the resulting litigation. With the help of her brother-in-law Philip Barton Key, Rebecca arranged partial payments on her most pressing obligations and hoped the farmstead would not have to be sold or subdivided for the rest.

Rebecca's was not an uncommon dilemma. Forrest and his contemporaries were products of an age when transactions were made in good faith, often consummated by a handshake, a promise to pay and—where land was involved—to convey at a later date. Conveyances made were frequently improperly surveyed and recorded. Record keeping was especially unstructured in the area of the Federal City project.

When problems caused by such transactions arose, they were settled in the Circuit Court of the District of Columbia, of which Forrest had been the first clerk. Probably with his court experience in mind and with characteristic integrity, he not only made provisions in his will for those errors he knew could arise from his land transfers but directed that his estate take the responsibility for those errors that might surface in years to come. Unfortunately he did not foresee the continuing devaluation of his holdings; and he underestimated the extent of his indebtedness and the ability of his estate to pay.

Philip Barton Key's death in 1815 deprived Rebecca of a good and valuable friend, but at the same time gave her an opportunity to save Rosedale. Although Key died intestate, he left a written declaration that upon his death Rosedale, its 126 1/2 acres, and those furnishings that had been mortgaged to him by Uriah Forrest were to become the property of Rebecca and her heirs forever.

With the mortgage on her holdings thus discharged, Rebecca was free to sell furniture, slaves, and livestock. Even though she now owned the farm, she found she could not raise enough money to maintain it; nor could she interest her children, grown and busy with their own lives, to take that responsibility. She chose to leave her home to tenants and rent a house in Georgetown, where she lived with her one remaining servant, Caroline, and Caroline's small children. Meanwhile, Rosedale languished with only intermittent tenants to keep it in temporary care.

Rebecca found financial relief in 1838 under the country's first Pension Act for Widows of War Veterans. She was awarded a monthly stipend plus a retroactive sum of $600, which enabled her to complete the purchase of a small brick house in Georgetown and live in modest comfort the rest of her days (figs. 19, 20). Contributing to her peace of mind was the rescue of Rosedale by her daughter Ann.

Fig. 20. *Georgetown Home of Rebecca Forrest.* Early nineteenth-century town house. Originally freestanding with an extra lot at the corner of West and Washington Streets (30th and P). Currently in a row of houses. Facade moderately altered. (Photograph by author)

Ann married John Green, a veteran of the United States Navy who had served under Commodore Stephen Decatur in the War of 1812. The ceremony took place on November 13, 1817, in the parlor at Rosedale. The couple established a home in the city of Washington. As Ann's family increased, she and John Green accepted Rebecca's offer to live at the farm. It was they who made Rosedale a home again (fig. 21):

The once-thriving country estate had deteriorated. The house was dilapidated, the grounds overgrown and snake infested. Cleared and planted, repaired and painted, Rosedale renewed became what it had been in Ann's childhood—a working farm and a hospitable home where again notables gathered, such as President James Madison and his wife, the irrepressible Dolley Madison.

Rebecca Plater Forrest died in 1843 at her Georgetown home and was buried beside her husband in the family plot at the Presbyterian Burial Ground in Georgetown. Her eldest daughter, Elizabeth, who married Upton Read of Runnymeade, had died in 1817, and Elizabeth's only child shortly thereafter. Maria first married the wealthy John Tayloe of Mt. Airy, Virginia. She was widowed and married the second time to Dr. Benjamin Bohrer. Rebecca's two sons, Benjamin Stoddert Forrest and George Plater Forrest had predeceased her. Both died without issue, terminating by name the lineage of Rebecca and Uriah Forrest. Rebecca's home of origin, Sotterley, had been lost in a game of dice by her nephew, George Plater V. Rosedale alone was left to carry on the family heritage.

In her will, Rebecca gave Rosedale, its tract of land and buildings, to daughter Ann Forrest Green for her "sole and separate use . . . free of any interest or control of her husband."

Ann not only saved and improved Rosedale but restored vitality to the family name and reputation. She was a cheerful composite of her parents, blending the best characteristics of both with her own individual strength. Small in stature, Ann was courageous, innovative, and insightful. She met the challenges of running a farm, managing a household of ten children, leading an active social, cultural, and community life, while at the same time caring for her ailing husband, who died in 1850.

Ann Forrest was the leader in the establishment of a Catholic congregation in nearby Tenleytown. She was considered the most active

Fig. 21. *Mr. and Mrs. John (Ann Forrest) Green*. Nineteenth-century owners of Rosedale. (Forrest-Rosedale Collection)

lay worker for the early church and was therefore accorded "the privilege of selecting its name." Ann Forrest Green unabashedly chose her own name, christening the religious edifice St. Ann's Church, by which it is known today.

The Green family was often noted in the press, notoriety that was sometimes unwelcome, especially during an episode involving Mexico's Emperor Maximilian. In 1862, Ann's young daughter Alice married the diplomat Don Angelo Iturbide, son of Don Augustine Iturbide, the first emperor of Mexico. The wedding, held in the drawing room of Rosedale, was acclaimed as a marriage of international importance. When the groom's father was deposed and executed, his replacement, Emperor Maximilian, an Austrian with no heirs of his own, asked to adopt Alice and Angelo's firstborn, a son named Augustine after his grandfather. Beguiled by promises of titles and benefits befitting their child's royal blood, the young couple agreed to the emperor's request.

Upon reflection, the impetuous Iturbides changed their minds and attempted to regain their son. After a long, much publicized struggle that included the intervention of the secretary of state, William Seward, the emperor returned the child to his parents.

During the American Civil War, Washington was protected by a ring of fully manned forts. Union soldiers, stationed at Fort Reno, near Tenleytown, were given food and water by the local residents. Absent documentation, it is said that care and shelter for wounded and ill servicemen were provided at Rosedale.

In 1865, Ann Green gave her son George 23 1/2 acres of choice land to the south and in front of the residence between today's Newark Street and Woodley Road. Near today's Macomb street George built Forrest Hill, a two-story house of local stone—simple in design, oblong in shape, and topped by a hip roof.

In May 1886, George Green sold Forrest Hill, then composed of 28 acres, to President Grover Cleveland as a summer residence for himself and his bride-to-be, Frances Folsom. The house was chosen for the same reasons the Forrests and Greens chose the Rosedale site—the lure of a rural environment, fresh air, clear water, an excellent view, and an ideal refuge from the busy city.

President Cleveland remodeled the house in the new turn-of-the-century Victorian fashion. He covered the stone exterior with wooden

Fig. 22. *President Grover Cleveland's Country House, Red Top*, ca. 1886. Drawing by Hughson Hawley from Peter and Southwick, *Cleveland Park*.

Fig. 23. *Photograph of Mrs. Cazenove Lee*, standing on the spot where President Cleveland's "Red Top" was located. Her home is in the background. (*Washington Post*, March 15, 1959). See p. 79.

additions, double porches, balconies, cupolas, turrets, second-floor galleries with blind arches and fanciful exterior trim. The roof was painted red. Forrest Hill, renamed Oak View by the president, was popularly known as Red Top (figs. 22, 23).

The president and his young wife added to the vivacity and fame of the original residents of Rosedale. Frances Folsom was a college-educated, independent, liberal woman who set her own standards. She declined to wear a bustle at a time when other women would not dare to be seen without one. She wore straw turbans instead of the traditional bonnets. She felt free to walk unescorted through the fields to attend the little wooden Episcopal church of St. Alban's on the hill across Woodley Road. (fig. 24) As the children of Rosedale picked cherries from the trees that separated the Forrest and Cleveland estates, the First Lady would stop to visit and politely ask to taste the fruit. Her youth and candor delighted residents. It is said that a road on the east side of Rosedale (34th Place) was originally named Folsom Place in her honor.

Fig. 24. *St. Alban's Wooden Church, 1896*. Located on the Georgetown to Frederick Road (Wisconsin Avenue). It was here that Mrs. Grover Cleveland attended the church services of the Reverend J. Neilson Falls. (Committee on History, *The Story of St. Alban's Parish*)

When Ann Forrest Green died on September 13, 1870, she left her property of approximately 100 acres to her children. After Ann's death, a new age began in old Pretty Prospects. In the closing years of the nineteenth century country estates diminished and communities developed.

Resistance to Washington, D.C., as a permanent capital of the United States had all but disappeared. Government institutions and buildings multiplied, accompanied by a growth in population. Development beyond what had been the original northern boundary of the early city—Boundary Street (Florida Avenue) increased, especially toward the north and west, the vicinity of Pretty Prospects and Rosedale.

After President Cleveland's defeat for reelection, he sold Red Top to Senator Francis G. Newlands of Nevada, the real estate entrepreneur responsible for building the suburb of Chevy Chase in Montgomery County, Maryland. He and other senators sponsored a bill providing for an expansion of the District of Columbia's street system to accelerate development. The bill included funding for the assistance of Frederick Law Olmstead, a well-known landscape planner. Two major avenues were laid out to facilitate travel to the newly forming suburban areas: Wisconsin Avenue (the old Georgetown to Frederick Road) was constructed in 1890, followed by Connecticut Avenue in 1892. The deep gullies of Rock Creek were bridged, and tracks for electric streetcars were installed. Rock Creek was purchased by the federal government as a national park, increasing the desirability of its abutting lands.

When the Naval Observatory was moved to its present location on Massachusetts Avenue in the 1890s, employees sought homes for themselves and their families nearby. Miss Flora Brown recalled that her father, William Murphy Brown—an astronomical computer at the observatory—persuaded Charles Nourse at the Highlands to rent them the small stone cottage at the rear of his property. It had been built years before for a retired "colored couple." Once enlarged, it was comfortable for the Browns and their six children. The cottage is now the Field House of the Hearst Playground located behind the Sidwell Friends School.

Miss Flora grew up as the community of Cleveland Park (named after the president) was developing. John Sherman, one of the early architects in the Park, was a member of St. Alban's Episcopal Church, as were the Browns. Miss Flora remembered when the only streets were Woodley Lane, part of Newark Street, Pierce Mill Road (now Tilden Street), and Wisconsin and Connecticut avenues. She recalled seeing her first automobile in 1896, an "open Ford" stuck on Wisconsin Avenue. When the machine stopped and the owner was not able to restart it, incredulous neighbors, including Miss Flora, gathered to watch.

The Brown children were educated at the new Tenleytown Public Elementary School. For recreation, there were church and civic festivities, but for the most part, young people walked, picnicked, and swam in Rock Creek, especially in the area of Pierce's Mill, and hiked or rode the trolley to the Chesapeake and Ohio Canal to watch the barges come and go.

Forrest-Green heirs slowly partitioned and sold Rosedale's outer acreage to eager developers. Early development began on the high ground east of the Rosedale residence on Highland Place, Newark Street, 34th Street, and 34th Place, with houses built in the full flowery style of Victorian eclecticism.

Although it was costly to maintain, the Forrest-Green family was reluctant to sell the residence or its immediate grounds. Unmarried and widowed aunts lived at Rosedale; nephews, nieces, and cousins summered there; and, when the owners were financially pressed, the property was rented. The old house had not been modernized and was still without electricity and heat. The roof leaked and the grounds needed attention. One widowed Forrest descendant, Mrs. Louisa Key Norton, after whom Cleveland Park's Norton Place was named, admitted that she preferred to move to the Grafton Apartments in Washington where it was nice and warm and where there was "sociability."

On October 17, 1917, Mr. and Mrs. Avery Coonley of Chicago, newcomers to Washington, were searching for a place to live. After seeing Rosedale, which was available to rent at that time, they made a tempting provisional offer of purchase to the Forrest-Green family. They agreed to rent the property "for several years" for $12,000 and to improve the house and its 8.66 acres during their tenancy, with the option to buy for the sum of $80,000. Their offer was accepted.

The Coonleys were a prominent Chicago family. In 1908, they had commissioned the nationally known architect Frank Lloyd Wright to build one of his famed prairie-style houses as their residence in Riverside, Illinois. When Wright visited Rosedale, his friend and patron Mrs. Coonley asked him what he thought of the architecture of the Forrest house, which was, she pointed out "different, and not exactly what you designed for me at Riverside." "No," he agreed, "but it is honest" and "good for its time."

The new family enjoyed the "charming old house." Mr. and Mrs. Coonley were dedicated Christian Scientists. Mrs. Coonley was a practitioner, and her husband, the head of a new Committee on Publications of the Church of Christ, Scientist, District of Columbia. Their daughter Elizabeth was nearly fifteen years old when her family moved to Rosedale. She remembered that her parents were attracted to the estate because of its old-fashioned ambience and because it had a stable "fit for a gentleman's horses." Her father was an ardent horseman. He rode in Rock Creek Park before breakfast, after which he drove to work behind a team of gaited Kentucky horses.

The Coonleys adjusted to their new home in Washington, although it was the first time Mrs. Coonley and her daughter had been called "honey" by clerks in a department store. They improved Rosedale by installing hot water heat and electricity. They repaired and restored the termite-ridden portions of the residence rather than demolish the structure—as had been recommended. They painted the exterior, carefully choosing the "right yellow." Additional rockers were placed on the front porch, prompting their maid to say the house looked like an old hotel!

Mr. and Mrs. Coonley preferred to preserve the general character of Rosedale and not to revise it. They landscaped the grounds, replacing dead trees and shrubs; they planted redbud and added a pine walk along the east boundary of the estate. They repaired rose trellises and grape arbors. In the grape arbor on the 36th Street side there was a small semicircular pool. There they placed a bronze statue of Pan, a rural deity of Greek and Roman mythology—god of the woods, fields, and flocks. Daughter Elizabeth felt that the little faun, part beast and part man, seemed to play his reed pipes to serenade the garden, the grape arbor, and the pool.

The Coonleys built a frame guesthouse (painted yellow), tennis courts, a gazebo, and a new greenhouse. They planted a large vegetable garden on the Ordway Street side. For livestock other than riding horses, they kept a cow named Rose, chickens, and a plow horse called Gypsy Dare.

Avery Coonley died at Rosedale in April 1920. His widow Queene Ferry Coonley purchased the estate in the fall of the same year, becoming the first owner of Rosedale other than Uriah Forrest and his descendants. The Coonley daughter Elizabeth married the distinguished Washington architect Waldron Faulkner at Rosedale. Her husband built a large brick home in the "Grecian mode" as their residence and a smaller, somewhat similar one beside it on the west side of the grounds at 36th Street. When Mrs. Coonley died in 1958, she willed Rosedale to her daughter and husband, who rented the property to Mr. and Mrs. John Irwin II.

In 1959, the Waldron Faulkners sold Rosedale and 6.7 acres to the nearby National Cathedral (the Protestant Episcopal Cathedral Foundation of the District of Columbia) as a boarding facility for students from their school for girls. Before the transaction Winthrop Faulkner, architect son of Waldron, acquired a strip of the land on the Ordway Street side of Rosedale, where he built two modern masonry residences.

The grounds of Rosedale had become an oasis, a private park for nearby residents. Considerate neighbors were permitted to enjoy the grounds during the nearly forty-year Coonley-Faulkner ownership. Mrs. Coonley, an educator and philanthropist, appreciated the historic significance of the house and occasionally gave informal tours of the property (fig. 25).

Her daughter continued the tradition. Mrs. Elizabeth Faulkner

Fig. 25. *Mrs. Avery Coonley with Family and Friends, Rosedale* 1954. Front row seated, Mrs. Waldron (Elizabeth) Faulkner, Mrs. Avery (Queene Ferry) Coonley, Mrs. Mary Faulkner (mother of Waldron). Second row standing, Waldron Faulkner between two friends, with daughter Celia Faulkner at the end. (Faulkner Family Collection)

participated in the Cleveland Park Community Library Committee's sponsorship of Grace Dunlap Peter and Joyce D. Southwick's *Cleveland Park: An Early Residential Neighborhood of the Nation's Capital*, the first book published that recognized the historic importance of Uriah Forrest's Rosedale and the part of Pretty Prospects that became Cleveland Park. The committee launched the publication with the first Cleveland Park House Tour on March 15, 1959. Rosedale was the stellar attraction.

Fearful that the old house might be demolished to accommodate the building plans of the new owners, the National Cathedral, the community formed the Cathedral-Rosedale Neighborhood Committee to discuss the matter. As a result, the purchasers promised to protect the historic house and its open setting in return for an uncontested zoning variance.

The National Cathedral School built three three-story dormitories, connected by glass and masonry corridors, behind Rosedale and on the east and west sides. Designed by the architectural firm of Faulkner, Fryer & Vanderpool, the modern red brick and concrete buildings encircled the comparatively small eighteenth-century yellow frame house like overprotective arms, obscuring the vista and the grounds except on the south (Newark Street) and a small triangle on the west (36th Street). The house was utilized by the staff (fig. 26).

By 1977 boarding schools for girls were no longer popular, and the Cathedral sold Rosedale and a 6-acre tract to Youth for Understanding, a nonprofit international student exchange organization, for its administrative headquarters. The dormitories now serve as offices, and the house is used as a residence for staff and guests. This sale was made after neighbors protested a possible sale to the Bulgarian Socialist Republic for an embassy. Architect Winthrop Faulkner bought the piece of land facing 36th Street, where he built three modern brick residences.

General Uriah Forrest's eighteenth-century frame farmhouse, threatened by demolition, its grounds diminished by development, survives. It is crowded, less visible, but enduring, a small yellow beacon on a hill reflecting the pages of our country's dramatic past and lighting

3501 Newark Street, N.W.
Washington, DC

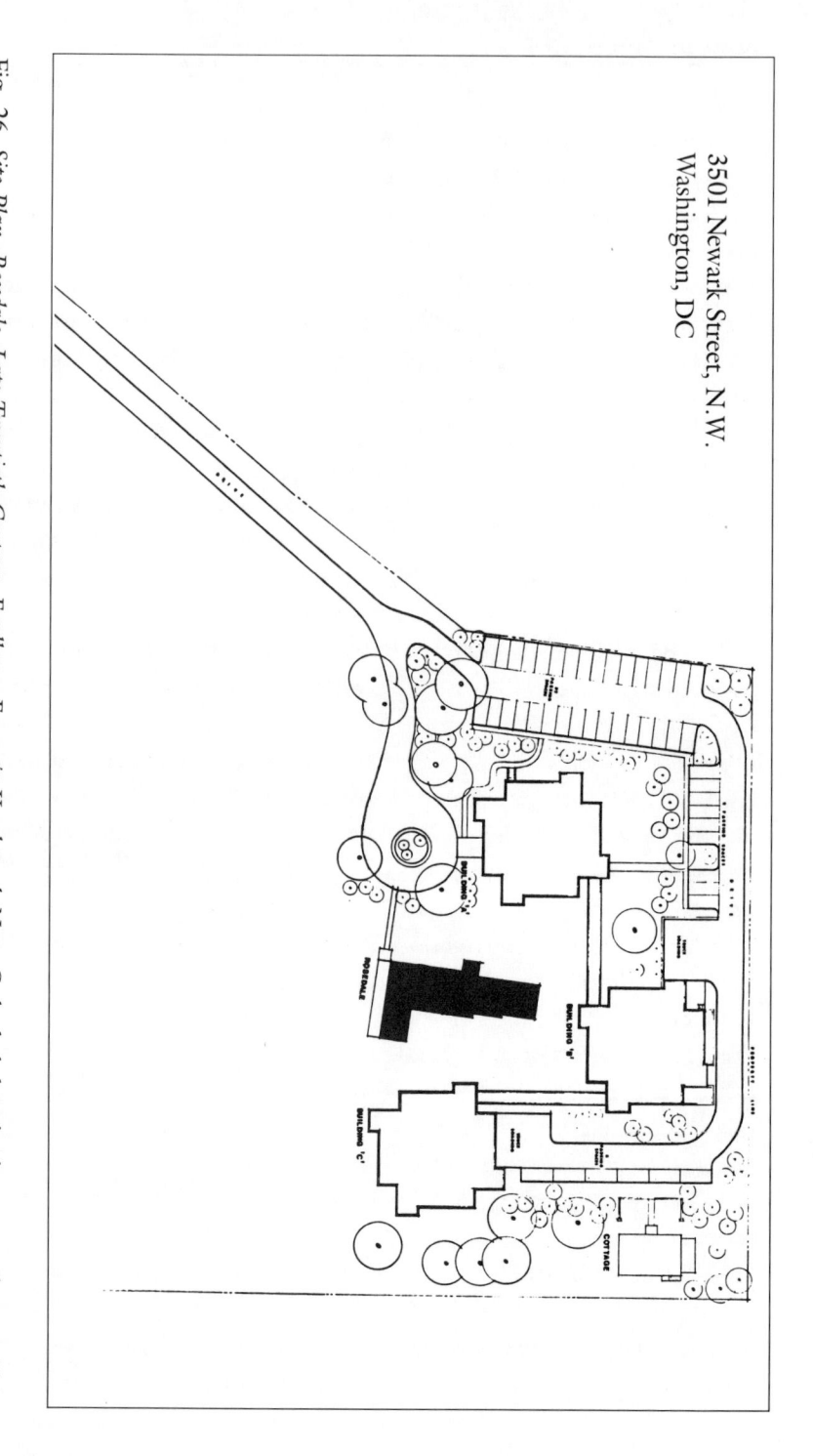

Fig. 26. *Site Plan, Rosedale, Late Twentieth Century*, Faulkner, Fryer & Vanderpool. Note Cathedral dormitories, connecting corridors, parking lot. (Courtesy Youth for Understanding)

a path for its future. The future of Rosedale improves with the recognition of its historic identity. It is a designated historic landmark on the National Register of Historic Places; it is part of the neighborhood of Cleveland Park that has recently been designated as a historic district; and a local historical society has been formed. The vigilance of its devoted following in Cleveland Park such as the Friends of Rosedale, and the enlightened stewardship of the present owners, Youth for Understanding, should protect it from further change.

No old house would be complete without a ghost, and Rosedale has several. There are stories of a secret passageway behind the stairs leading to the loft of the stone cottages, meant for mysterious exits and entrances. There are unexplained sounds and footsteps in the residence. A rocking chair in the parlor, where General Uriah Forrest died in 1805, rocks when no visible presence is seated in it. And there is a beautiful female figure in a long, flowing white gown who has been seen in the hallways and on the stairs. One evening, in the presence of witnesses, the front door opened as if by an invisible hand, through which the same white-robed figure moved silently onto Rosedale's moonlit verandah.

Fig. 27. *Bronze Statue of Pan.* Doorway of Herb Cottage, National Cathedral. Drawing by Babs Gaillard from sculpture by Edith Barretto Parsons. (Permission of the artist)

Sources And Notes

The author's original research—found in Louise Mann Madden and Sheila Dressner Ruffine, eds., *Cleveland Park: Washington, D.C. Neighborhood Research*, rev. ed. (Washington, D.C.: American University, 1977); Sarah White Hamilton, Louise Mann Madden, and Sheila Dressner Ruffine, eds., *Historic Preservation Study of Cleveland Park, Washington, D.C.* (Washington, D.C.: By the editors, 1977); and Louise Mann-Kenney, "Biography of Uriah Forrest," unpublished—is incorporated throughout.

Sources are listed by chapter; comments by page; and lengthy titles are abbreviated when repeated. Abbreviations most frequently used are: LC: Library of Congress, Washington, D.C.; MCHS: Montgomery County Historical Society, Rockville, Md.; *MHM*: *Maryland Historical Magazine*; MHS: Maryland Historical Society, Baltimore; NA: National Archives, Washington, D.C.; *RCHS: Records of the Columbia Historical Society*, Washington, D.C.; SMCHS: St. Mary's County Historical Society, Leonardtown, Md.

CHAPTER I

SOURCES

Chapter I is based on the following sources:

State and Local Archives: Archives of the State of Maryland, Hall of Records, Annapolis, Md.; Colonial Dames, Washington, D.C.; Columbia Historical Society, Washington, D.C.; Daughters of the American Revolution, Washington D.C.; Lloyd House, Alexandria, Va.; MCHS, Rockville, Md.; MHS, Baltimore, Md.; Oak Hill Cemetery register, Washington, D.C.; Pennsylvania Historical Society, Philadelphia, Pa.; Sotterley Archives, Sotterley Mansion, Inc., Hollywood, Md.; SMCHS, Leonardtown, Md.

Land Records and Tax Assessments: D.C. Office of the Recorder of Deeds, Washington, D.C.; MCHS, Rockville, Md.; Rockville Court House, Rockville, Md.

Church Records and Journals: Robert Barnes, comp., *Marriages and Deaths from the Maryland Gazette, 1727-1839* (Baltimore: G. P. Publishing Co., 1976); Henry J. Berkley, "Early Records of the Church and Parish of All Faiths, St. Mary's County, Maryland" *MHM* 30 (1935): 326-63; 31 (1935): 16-36; Margaret King Fresco, *Marriages and Deaths St. Mary's County, Maryland, 1634-1900* (By the author, 1982); Register of St. Andrew's Episcopal Church, Leonardtown, Md.

Family Histories: Wesley Armor, *Ancestral Records from the 17th to the 20th Centuries* (By the author, 1971); Maria Green Devereux, "Family History," 1881, unpublished, author's files; Margaret King Fresco, Forrest genealogy, unpublished, author's files, "The Forrest Family," SMCHS, *Chronicles of St. Mary's* 161, no. 12 (1968): 243-44, "Colonel Uriah Forrest," oral presentation, Daughters of the American Revolution, January 17, 1976, author's files; and author's personal interviews; George T. Kearsley, "The Kearsley Family in America," 1911, LC, Local History and Genealogy, C.S. 71, K24; Isabel Green Zantzinger, "Pretty Prospect," *National Cathedral School News* 19, no. 2 (1965): 14-20. See also Grace Dunlap Peter and Joyce D. Southwick, *Cleveland Park: An Early Residential Neighborhood of the Nation's Capital* (Washington, D.C.: Cleveland Park Library Committee, 1958).

General Directories: *Dictionary of American Biography* (New York: Charles Scribner and Sons, 1934); James L. Harrison et al., comps., *Biographical Dictionary of the American Congress, 1774-1949* (Washington, D.C.: Government Printing Office, 1950), pp. 39, 57, 1173; Edward C. Papenfuse et al., *Biographical Dictionary of the Maryland Legislature, 1653-1790* (Baltimore: Johns Hopkins University Press, 1979), pp. 647, 648; Ransom B. True, *Biographical Dictionary of Early Virginia, 1607-1660* (Jamestown, Va.: Association for the Preservation of Virginia Antiquities, n.d.).

Forrest's Revolutionary War Records: Archives of Maryland, Hall of Records, Annapolis, Md., 1776-1781; Edwin Beitzell, *St. Mary's County in the American Revolution, Calendar of Events* (Leonardtown, Md.: St. Mary's County Bicentennial Commission, 1975); NA, RG 15, 93, Veteran's Administration, Revolutionary War and Pension file, Uriah Forrest, W.24225, and RG 360, Miscellaneous Manuscripts and Records of the Continental Congress and the Revolutionary War; J.

Thomas Scharf, *History of Maryland* (1897; reprint, Hatboro, Pa.: Tradition Press, 1967); Charles Coleman Sellers, *Charles Willson Peale* (Philadelphia, Pa.: American Philosophical Society, 1947), p. 170.

Consignment Merchant Material: Allen C. Clark, "Daniel Carrol of Duddington," *RCHS* 39 (1938): 4; Richard K. MacMaster, "The Tobacco Traders in France, Letters of Joseph Fenwick," *RCHS* 60, 1 (1965): 26-55, and "Georgetown and the Tobacco Trade, 1751-1783," *RCHS* 66 (1966-68): 33; Jacob M. Price, "One Family's Empire: The Russell-Lee-Clerk-Connection in Maryland, Britain, and India, 1707-1857," *MHM* 72, no. 2 (1979): 165-225; Benjamin Stoddert Letters, March 26, 1783, May 13, January 14, 1786, LC, Miscellaneous Manuscripts; The Tobacco Book, 1783-89, MHS Manuscripts, no. 1690.

The Federal City, Georgetown, and the Forrest-Marbury House: Janice Artemel et al., "Georgetown Waterfront Park," 1987, unpublished, Engineering Science, Inc., Washington, D.C., p. 60; Kenneth R. Bowling, *Creating the Federal City, 1774-1800: Potomac Fever* (Washington, D.C.: American Institute of Architects Press, 1988); D.C. Office of the Recorder of Deeds, Liber C-3 fol. 107, G7-A; Deering Davis et al., *Georgetown Houses of the Federal Period: Washington, D.C., 1780-1830* (New York: Bonanza Books, 1944), pp. 118, 121; Brook Farquar, *Montgomery County, Maryland, Old Homes and History, 1776-1952* (Baltimore: Monumental Printing Co., 1952), pp. 345-49; Robert Lyle and Edith Ray Saul, "The Forrest-Marbury House," unpublished, Peabody Room, Georgetown Library; Montgomery County Land Records, Rockville, Md., Courthouse, C-3-161; studies by M.M.P. International, Inc., the company that owns and has recently restored the Forrest-Marbury House; Tax Assessments of Georgetown and the Lower Potomac 100, 1793-1800, MCHS.

Residence Bill: 1 Stat. 130; Wilhelmus Bogart Bryan, *A History of the National Capital* (New York: MacMillan Co., 1914), p. 119.

Rosedale and Pretty Prospects Land Descriptions: Federal Writers Project, Works Progress Administration, American Guide Series, *Washington, City and Capital* (Washington, D.C.: Government Printing Office, 1937), pp. 13-15; Robert L. Humphrey and Mary Elizabeth Chambers, *Ancient Washington, American Indian Cultures of the Potomac*

Valley, G.W. Studies 6 (Washington, D.C.: George Washington University, 1977), pp. 7-10, 11-16, 17-23, Fig. 1 on p. ii; Junior League of Washington, *An Illustrated History of the City of Washington*, ed. Thomas Froncek (New York: Alfred A. Knopf, 1987); S. S. Mackall, *Early Days of Washington* (1899; reprint, Sterling, Ill.: Bishop Printing Co., 1934); author's personal knowledge.

Land Grant Material: H. Paul Caemmerer, *Washington: The Nation's Capital*, Senate Document 331, 7th Cong., 3d Sess. (Washington, D.C.: Government Printing Office, 1932); D.C. Office of the Recorder of Deeds; Bessie Wilmarth Gahn, *Original Patentees of Land at Washington, D.C., Prior to 1700* (By the author, 1936); Priscilla McNeil, "Pretty Prospects, A Study of a Land Grant," unpublished, author's files; Montgomery County Tax Assessments and Deeds, 1795-1802, MCHS; Hugh Taggart, "Old Georgetown," *RCHS* 11 (1908): 120-224; Walter Muir Whitehill, *Dumbarton Oaks, 1800-1966* (Cambridge, Mass.: Belknap Press of Harvard University Press, 1966), pp. 1-5.

Physical Description of the Cottage: Author's personal study, supplemented by advice and assistance from Max Darrow, Organization Director, Youth for Understanding, Rosedale; Faulkner Design Partnership, "Renovation Report, Rosedale Residence," September 1984; Geoffrey M. Gyrisco, "Archaeology at Rosedale" (Washington, D.C.: D.C. Historic Preservation Office, 1981); Mills, Claggett, and Wening, Architects, Engineers, Planners, "Scope of Work Specifications for Rosedale," December 1978, Washington, D.C.

General Historical References: Bryan, *History of the National Capital*; John W. Caughey and Ernest R. May, *A History of the United States* (Chicago: Rand McNally & Co., 1964); Robert Coakley and Stetson Conn, *War of the American Revolution* (Washington, D.C.: Center of Military History, U.S. Army, 1975); Mary C. Gillette, *Army Medical Department, 1775-1818* (Washington, D.C.: Center of Military History, U.S. Army, 1981); Samuel Eliot Morison, *History of the American People* (New York: Oxford University Press, 1965); Hester Daisey Richardson, *Sidelights on Maryland History with Sketches of Early Maryland Families* (Baltimore: Baltimore Genealogical Co., 1967);

Scharf, *History of Maryland*; Richard Walsh and William L. Fox, *Provincial Maryland: A History, 1632-1974* (Baltimore: MHS, 1974).

NOTES
Page 1
   The origin of the name Rosedale has been lost in history. There is no documentation to support the belief that Rosedale was the name of the Forrest family home in England. Josephus Nelson, specialist in the study of English country homes, LC, has found nothing to substantiate Rosedale's English antecedents; nor could he find an English country home named Rosedale.
   Although the estate was located within the 1791 boundary of the Territory of Columbia (later known as the District of Columbia), Maryland laws remained in force and residents considered themselves Marylanders.
   On May 8, 1973, Rosedale was designated a Category II Landmark on the National Register of Historic Places, a category defined as "Historic Landmarks and Historic Districts of value which contribute significantly to the cultural heritage or visual beauty and interest of the District of Columbia and its environs and which should be preserved or restored, if possible." The Joint Committee on Landmarks of the National Capital has recently eliminated numbered categories, replacing them with a general landmark status.
   The original boundaries of Cleveland Park are defined on a survey recorded in the D.C. Office of the Surveyor, Washington, D.C., Liber 9, fol. 71.

Page 2
   Forrest's firm is generally referred to as Forrest & Stoddert and occasionally as Forrest, Stoddert & Murdock. Although John Murdock, a wealthy Georgetowner, may have been a partner, the author has been unable to find eighteenth-century documentation confirming his status and his involvement in the business.
   The Forrest-Marbury House is named after its first two illustrious owners. On December 6, 1800, the house was purchased as a residence

by William Marbury. D.C. Office of the Recorder of Deeds, Liber C-3, fol. 107. Although owned, and probably built by both Forrest and Stoddert in the late 1780s, the deed was recorded in Stoddert's name alone, a practice not unusual for the partners. Montgomery County Land Records, C-3-161. The degree of the partners' participation in the building process of the Forrest house is not known.

Page 4

Descriptions of Sotterley are based on *Sotterley, St. Mary's County, Maryland* (Hollywood, Md.: Sotterley Mansion Foundation, Inc., n.d.), pp. 3-9; Sotterley Archives; Daniel Boorstin, ed. *Visiting Our Past: America's Historylands* (Washington, D.C.: National Geographic Society, 1977), pp. 112, 113; author's on-site observation.

Washington's diary entries are in John C. Fitzpatrick, ed., *Diaries of George Washington, 1748-1799* (Boston and New York: Houghton Mifflin Co., 1925), 4:153-55.

Suter's Tavern is no longer extant. Additional information is in Oliver W. Holmes, *Suter's Tavern, Birthplace of the Federal City* (Charlottesville, Va.: University Press of Virginia, 1973-74).

Page 5

Mrs. Stoddert's impressions of Georgetown are found in Benjamin Stoddert Letters, LC, Miscellaneous Manuscripts. Forrest and Stoddert were friends as well as business partners. In 1789, Stoddert named his son Benjamin Forrest Stoddert.

Pretty Prospects, the original name, was shortened over the years to Pretty Prospect. Letters of agreement for the property, February 6, 11, 1792, were signed by George Beall, William Deakins, and "General" Benjamin Stoddert. The deed and the 1793 survey for the property were in Stoddert's name only. This recurring error was corrected on documents as Uriah Forrest transferred portions of his land. D.C. Office of the Recorder of Deeds, Liber A-1-A, fols. 255-57, Liber B-2, fols. 31, 124, 129; Montgomery County Land Records, Liber D, fol. 174; Archives of Maryland, Hall of Records, Liber I-C-G, fol. 489.

Sources And Notes 69

Page 6

Today's Wisconsin Avenue follows the original Indian trail north from the Potomac River. Still the major artery from Georgetown inland, it has been known by various names through the years—the Rolling Road, Braddock's Road, the Great Road, the Georgetown to Frederick Road, the Tennally Town Road, and the Rockville Turnpike. For further information, see Judith Beck Helm, *Tenleytown, D.C.* (Washington, D.C.: Tennally Press, 1981), pp. 4, 23-25, 36, 65, 66.

Pierre L'Enfant's letter to Thomas Jefferson is found in H. Paul Caemmerer, *Life of Pierre Charles L'Enfant* (Washington, D.C.: National Republic Publishing Co., 1952), p. 136. For further information, see Elizabeth Kite, *L'Enfant and Washington* (Baltimore: Johns Hopkins University Press, 1929). James Kent's handwritten notes are on the margin of Thomas Lear's map of the city of Washington, published in Junior League of Washington, *Illustrated History of the City of Washington*, p. 37.

Page 11

The famous black squirrels of Cleveland Park are not indigenous but are twentieth-century newcomers whose lineage is probably traceable to the wild black Canadian squirrels that escaped from the National Zoo, 1902-06. Lynn Teo Simarski, "Tales of D.C.'s Colorful Squirrels Tell Background of Who's Hue," *Washington Post*, August 6, 1987, sec. D.C., p. 3.

CHAPTER II

SOURCES

Descriptions of Rosedale: Author's personal research, including on-site observations and measurements, aided by the professional studies acknowledged in Chapter I and the assistance of Max Darrow, Youth for Understanding; a series of interviews by the author with former residents, relatives, and guests, such as Mrs. Elizabeth Faulkner, daughter of Mr. and Mrs. Avery Coonley (twentieth-century owners of the estate), and Miss Ann Forrest Matthews and Mrs. Elizabeth Matthews Black (great-great-granddaughters of Uriah Forrest), who visited Rosedale as youngsters; also letters and notes of great-granddaughter, Mrs. Georgia Green West found in the Forrest family collection, and the published memoirs of great-great-granddaughter, Mrs. Isabel Green Zantzinger, *National Cathedral School News*; Peter and Southwick, *Cleveland Park*; nomination forms of the Joint Committee on Landmarks of the National Capital (for Rosedale, Woodley, and the Highlands); tax assessments of Georgetown, Lower Montgomery Counties, 1793 to 1798, MCHS. Details of Sotterley's history and inventories are found in Sotterley Archives; descriptions are the author's observations.

Forrest Construction Other Than Rosedale: Malcolm Vosburgh, "History of an Early Pair of Georgetown Houses," unpublished, author's files; William Buchanan, "Robert Morris, Seven Buildings," unpublished, author's files. See also Erastus Thatcher, *Founding of Washington City*, comp. from City Archives and District Records (Washington, D.C.: The Law Reporter Co., 1891); Sources and Notes, Chap. I, p. 2.

Furnishings at Rosedale—Interior and Exterior: Forrest's bankruptcy in 1802 required an official inventory of his assets and their location, providing a rare opportunity for information on Rosedale's exterior and interior furnishings. Sources are NA, RG 21, Inventory, Uriah Forrest, D.C. Inventories and Sales, vol. 1, 1799-1807; First Accounts, D.C. Accounts, 1802-19; D.C. Chancery Cases 300, Rule 2. Additions to the inventory appear in Gyrisco, "Archaeology at Rosedale"; announcements in local newspapers such as the *National Intelligencer and Washington Advertiser*, August-November 1802.

Furnishings listed were traced by the author, and, with the gracious cooperation of Forrest and Coonley descendants, some early artifacts of Rosedale were located and are described and illustrated. They have been authenticated by professional appraisers.

Information on food and menus may be found in most social histories of the period. Specific references for the text are Jonathan Susskind, "Constitutional Cooking," *News/Sentinel* (Palm Beach, Fla.), July 1, 2, 1987; Grace Dunlap Ecker, *A Portrait of Old George Town* (Richmond, Va.: Dietz Press, 1951), p. 93.

Sources And Notes

NOTES

Page 15

There is presently no information to explain why the house was built in sections, in what order, and in what time frame. While it is known that Rosedale was painted yellow prior to the Coonley occupation, early information regarding its color is not available. It is possible that Rosedale was originally yellow, for it was a popular color in the District of Columbia in the late eighteenth and early nineteenth centuries.

The side porch was removed by architect Waldron Faulkner, son-in-law of Mr. and Mrs. Avery Coonley, twentieth-century owners of Rosedale. Some repairs and modifications were necessitated by termite damage to the wood. The Coonleys once considered demolition of the structure because of this problem. Interviews with Mrs. Elizabeth Faulkner, Coonley daughter, 1984; Mr. Winthrop Faulkner, Coonley grandson, 1987.

Page 21

The bowl and pitcher are in the possession of Uriah Forrest's great-great-granddaughters Miss Ann Forrest Matthews and Mrs. Elizabeth Matthews Black and were examined and photographed by the author.

The Forrest silver, except for several items pictured in the text, was stolen from the Georgetown home of Mrs. Georgia Green West, great-granddaughter of Rebecca and Uriah Forrest, in the 1930s.

The George Washington goblet, also stolen, was described to the author by Miss Ann Forrest Matthews and Mrs. Elizabeth Matthews Black.

The Forrest dining room table could have been made in America, **for** Americans cabinetmakers used pattern books from England. Many Hepplewhite designs were derived from George Hepplewhite, *Cabinet-Maker and Upholster's Guide* (London, 1778).

Page 23

The French clock, still in the possession of the Forrest family, was listed in the inventory for the marshal's sale in the *National Intelligencer and Washington Advertiser*, August-November 1802.

Page 28

For Forrest's asparagus roots see "Diary of Mrs. William Thornton, 1800," *RCHS* 10 (1907): 128.

The stepping stone appears to be a quern, a portable millstone, hand turned, a relic from the early mills on Rock Creek. Information on querns is available in Charles Harell and Allen Keller, *The Mill* (Tarrytown, N.Y.: Sleepy Hollow Restorations, 1977); miscellaneous pamphlets at Pierce Mill, Rock Creek Park.

CHAPTER III

SOURCES

Biographical Material: Bryan, *History of the National Capital*, pp. 171, 222-23, 337; Harrison et al., comps,. *Biographical Directory of the American Congress, 1774-1949*; Papenfuse et al., *Biographical Dictionary of the Maryland Legislature*, p. 325.

Forrest's Land Acquisitions: Artemel et al., "Georgetown Waterfront Park," p. 60; D.C. Office of the Recorder of Deeds; Montgomery County Tax Assessments, 1783 to 1793, MCHS; William P. Palmer, *Calendar of Virginia State Papers and Other Manuscripts from January 1, 1785 to July 2, 1789* (Richmond, Va.: Superintendent of Public Printing, 1884); Papenfuse et al., *Biographical Dictionary of the Maryland Legislature*, p. 325; Earl Gregg Swem, *Virginia Historical Index* (Roanoke, Va.: Stone Printing and Manufacturing Co., 1943); Thatcher, *Founding of Washington*.

Birth Dates and Names of the Forrest Children: Rebecca's Bible, presently in the possession of Miss Ann Forrest Matthews; cross-reference, Rebecca's 1843 pension application, NA, RG 15, Veteran's Administration, Revolutionary War, W.24225. Other Forrest and Plater family material is found in Devereux, "Family History"; *Dictionary of American Biography*; Montgomery County Land Records; Papenfuse et al., *Biographical Dictionary of the Maryland Legislature*; Peter and Southwick, *Cleveland Park*; private correspondence between George Plater IV and Uriah Forrest, Sotterley Archives. Richard Forrest's story is told by his aunt, Kate Kearney Henry, "Richard Forrest and His Times," *RCHS* 5 (1907): 87-95; "Diary of Mrs. Thornton, 1800"; Archives, Office of the Postmaster General, Washington, D.C.

Sources And Notes

Social Activities: In the absence of diaries and pertinent personal letters of Rebecca and Uriah Forrest, their social activities are found in the diaries and letters of contemporaries. Uriah Forrest's dinner for President Adams is noted in the "Diary of Mrs. William Thornton, 1800," p. 152; Bryan, *History of the National Capital*, p. 349. Forrest's friendship with Adams is found in Papers and Letters of John Adams, LC, Miscellaneous Manuscripts; Charles Francis Adams, *The Works of John Adams* (Boston: Little, Brown and Co., 1853), 8:546-47, 637-38, 645; John Alexander Carroll and Mary Wells Ashworth, *George Washington* (New York: Charles Scribner's Sons, 1957), 7:443, 443n, 597, 597n.; Merrill D. Peterson, *Thomas Jefferson* (New York: Oxford University Press, 1970), pp. 568-69. Forrest's relationship with L'Enfant and Ellicott, as well as with Washington himself, can be traced in John C. Fitzpatrick, ed., *The Writings of George Washington* (Washington, D.C.: Government Printing Office, 1939), 32:297, 308-9, 353, 356-57. For other social references, see Allen C. Clark, "Letters of Captain William Duncanson," Robert Morris to Captain Duncanson, *RCHS* 14 (1911): 16, 17; *Thomas Sim Lee Corner* (Washington, D.C.: Historic Georgetown, Inc., n.d.); Zantzinger, "Pretty Prospect."

General Forrest's Second Military Career: Papenfuse et al., *Biographical Dictionary of the Maryland Legislature*, pp. 324, 325; Scharf, *History of Maryland*, 2:483; See also Morison, *History of the American People*, pp. 342, 536; Richard B. Morris, ed., *Encyclopedia of American History* (New York: Harper and Brothers, 1961).

Proprietors Agreement, March 30, 1791: The complex agreement between proprietors and the government is simplified in the text. Details may be found in Allen C. Clark, "Origin of the Federal City," *RCHS* 35-36 (1935): 44-46; William Tindall, *The Establishment and Government of the District of Columbia* (Washington, D.C.: Government Printing Office, 1901);

Bankruptcies and Insolvencies: NA, RG 21, Minutes of the Circuit Court of the District of Columbia, Federal District Papers. Early writing on the District of Columbia's financial dilemma is in Bryan, *History of the National Capital*, pp. 219, 220, 298. Uriah Forrest's letter to the District Commissioners to forestall bankruptcy, March 28, 1801, is in

NA, RG 42, Federal District Papers, M-371. Additional information on Philip Barton Key's assistance to Uriah Forrest may be found in Peter and Southwick, *Cleveland Park*, pp. 18, 29; NA, RG 21, Chancery Records, Uriah Forrest, 133, July 27, 1807; NA, RG 21, Appearances, Trials and Judicials, nos. 194, 1023, Circuit Court, D.C., June 1801-March 1802; D.C. Office of the Recorder of Deeds, Libers F6 and H8, fol. 242. The *National Intelligencer and Washington Advertiser*, August 30-November 8, 1802, publicize the bankruptcy and marshal's sale.

The Maryland Loan: Fitzpatrick, ed., *Writings of George Washington*, 32:353, 356-57; Bryan, *History of the National Capital*, pp. 412-19.

Marbury v. Madison: Marbury v. *Madison*, 1 Cranch 137 (1803); Bryan, *History of the National Capital*, p. 410.

Forrest's Expenditures: NA, RG 21, D.C. Accounts, 1802-19, First Accounts, Uriah Forrest; D.C. Chancery Cases, 300, Rule 2, Uriah Forrest.

NOTES
Page 31

The announcement of the dissolution of the Forrest & Stoddert partnership appeared in the *Georgetown Weekly Ledger*, September 10, 1793. John Murdock's name was not mentioned. The Forrest-Stoddert friendship continued after the two had dissolved their shipping business. Uriah made purchases for Mrs. Stoddert at her request when he traveled to Annapolis. Benjamin Stoddert later became the first secretary of the United States Navy.

Page 33

Recognition of Forrest's qualifications for federal positions is found in Fitzpatrick, ed., *Writings of George Washington*, vols. 19, 31; Julian P. Boyd, ed., *The Papers of Thomas Jefferson* (Princeton, N.J.: Princeton University Press, 1953), vols. 12, 20.

Page 34

The Burr-Hamilton-Forrest story is told in Zantzinger, "Pretty Prospect."

Page 36

Syndicate members James Greenleaf, John Nicholson, and Robert Morris were sentenced to debtor's prison. John Nicholson died while incarcerated; James Greenleaf and Robert Morris survived and were later released.

The Bankruptcy Act of 1800 (2 Stat. 19) under which the petition against Uriah Forrest was filed was a legal landmark—a temporary measure designed to aid indebted members of the mercantile class and their creditors. (In the years to come, Congress would enact new laws for bankruptcy following major and minor economic depressions.) Based upon English law, it was in fact, more lenient in that the United States included exceptions, exemptions, and, most important, with the agreement of the creditors, discharge of the debtors' obligations. As in England, however, the procedure was involuntary. Although businessmen from Maryland, Pennsylvania, and New York made use of the act, it was most used and needed in the Federal District of Washington. See U.S. Constitution, Art. 1, sec. 8, clause 4; Richard Peter, *Public Statutes at Large, U.S.A.* (Boston: Charles C. Little and James Brown, 1854), 2:546; Vern Countryman, "A History of the American Bankruptcy Law," *Commercial Law Journal* 81 (1976): 226-29; Charles Warren, *Bankruptcy in United States History* (Cambridge, Mass.: Harvard University Press, 1965).

Page 38

The Federal District was divided into two counties by the Congress of the United States in 1801 (2 Stat. L, 105), the County of Washington on the Maryland side of the Potomac, and the County of Alexandria on the Virginia side. Alexandria County was re-ceded to Virginia in 1846. The boundaries of the early city of Washington (in Washington County) were approximately the Eastern Branch on the east, the Potomac River on the south, and Boundary Street (Florida Avenue) on the north. These boundaries were expanded, north, east, and west in 1871. Georgetown remained a separate city until 1895. At that time, Congress merged Georgetown with the City of Washington but neglected to dissolve the old County of Washington. The County of Washington is not to be confused with present-day Washington County,

Maryland. See Edward M. Douglas, *Boundaries, Areas, Geographic Centers and Altitudes of the United States and the Several States*, 2d ed. (Washington, D.C.: Government Printing Office, 1932) pp. 132-37; William Tindall, *The Establishment and Government of the District of Columbia* (Washington, D.C.: Government Printing Office, 1901); *The Government of the District of Columbia* and *Washington, City and Capital*, D.C. Government pamphlets, 1958, 1975.

CHAPTER IV

SOURCES AND NOTES

Medical and Funeral Bills: NA, RG 21, D.C. Accounts, First Accounts, Uriah Forrest; D.C. Chancery Cases, 300, Rule 2, Uriah Forrest. For general information on funeral practices, see Alice Morse Earle, *Home Life in Colonial Days* (Williamstown, Mass.: Calico House Publishers, 1984); Stephen J. Vicchio, "Baltimore Burial Practices, Mortuary Art and Notions of Grief and Bereavement, 1780-1900," *MHM* 81 (1986): 134-37; Bryan, *History of the National Capital*, pp. 67, 83, 607, 608.

Forrest's Physical Condition: Recollections of Devereux in Peter and Southwick *Cleveland Park*, p. 14. Miss Ann Forrest Matthews told the story of Uriah Forrest at the entrance gate of Rosedale in an interview by the author, 1986. Information about Dr. Worthington is found in Bryan, *History of the National Capital*, p. 324n; Ecker, *Portrait of Old George Town*, p. 115.

Uriah Forrest's Will, June 22, 1805: D.C. Office of the Register of Wills, Washington, D.C.

Presbyterian Burial Ground: Information found in the records of Oak Hill Cemetery, 30th and R streets, Georgetown, where the remains of Rebecca and Uriah Forrest were transferred in 1883 by the District Chapter of the Sons of the American Revolution. Although the Forrests were Episcopalians, they affiliated with the Georgetown Presbyterian Church. It was convenient, the pastor popular, and the congregation ecumenical.

Forrest's Obituary: Barnes, comp., *Marriages and Deaths from the Maryland Gazette*, p. 61; the later tribute is in Thomas J. Rogers, *A New American Biographical Dictionary or Remembrances of the Departed Heroes, Sages and Statesmen of America* (Easton, Md: Easton Press, 1824).

CHAPTER V

SOURCES

Philip Barton Key: Key's assistance to Rebecca is documented throughout the records of Forrest's first accounts: NA, RG 21, D.C. Accounts, and is discussed in Devereux, "Family History"; Peter and Southwick, *Cleveland Park*.

Wills, Pension, Death Notice: Wills of Uriah Forrest (June 22, 1805), Rebecca Forrest (June 10, 1843), and Ann Forrest Green (November 11, 1858), D.C. Office of the Register of Wills; Pension information: 5 Stat. 7 (1838); NA, RG 15, Veteran's Administration, Revolutionary War and Pension file, Uriah Forrest, W.24225; Rebecca Forrest's death notice appeared in the *National Intelligencer*, September 6, 1843.

Disposition of Sotterley: *Sotterley, St. Mary's County, Maryland*.

Biographical Data on the Family of John Green: Family bibles, genealogies, and recollections; Catholic Archdiocese of Washington, *St. Ann's Church* (South Hackensack, N.J.: Custombook, Inc., Ecclesiastical Color Publishers, 1969) p.4; Peter and Southwick, *Cleveland Park*; John Clagett Proctor, "Historic Landmarks of Cleveland Park," *Sunday Star* (Washington, D.C.), September 3, 1944, which includes a copy of the letter of intervention of Secretary of State William Seward.

Anecdotal History of the Clevelands, St. Albans, Rosedale, and Cleveland Park: History Committee, comp., *The Story of St. Alban's Parish, 1854-1929* (Baltimore: Monumental Printing Co., 1929); Peter and Southwick, *Cleveland Park*; interviews by the author with Miss Flora Brown, former librarian of St. Alban's Parish Church, Mrs. Elizabeth Faulkner, Miss Ann Forrest Matthews, and Mrs. Elizabeth Matthews Black.

Sale of Rosedale: The letter of the proposed purchase of Rosedale by the Coonleys is in the files of the Columbia Real Estate Title Insurance Company, Washington, D.C.; the deed of purchase, October 9, 1920, D.C. Office of the Recorder of Deeds, Liber 4373, fol. 411; the deed to the Protestant Episcopal Cathedral Foundation of the District of Columbia, July 31, 1959, D.C. Office of the Recorder of Deeds, Liber 11282, fol. 160; Statement of Principles Governing the Disposition of Rosedale, Agreed to by Bishop William F. Creighton for the Cathedral and Mrs. Gilbert Harrison for the Neighborhood Committee, November 30, 1966, author's files; deed to Youth for Understanding, Inc., a Michigan Corporation, June 28, 1977, D.C. Office of the Recorder of Deeds, doc. 20087.

NOTES
Page 47

Key's ownership of Rosedale land came by a circuitous route common to many property transactions of the period. In February 1800, Uriah Forrest mortgaged 420 acres, "on which my dwelling house stands" to the state of Maryland as part of the personal security required by the state for a $50,000 loan to the Federal City. In June 1801, Uriah Forrest mortgaged the same property to John Templeman, a Georgetown businessman, as part of a complex financial settlement, possibly because he had prior information that the Treasury Department would take over the series of Maryland loans, an official decision made in 1802. The suit against Forrest by the state of Maryland was canceled in April 1802. When Key bought the property from Templeman is not clear, but in a directive to be followed after his death, Key returned to Rebecca Negroes, plate, and furniture he had mortgaged from Uriah Forrest before his bankruptcy, and the 126 1/2 acres on which "the widow lives," in return for a corner house in Georgetown that Key bought from Uriah Forrest but was never conveyed to him. D.C. Office of the Recorder of Deeds, Liber G, fol. 141, Liber F6, Liber H8; NA, RG 21, no. 69, Trials, July term, 1802, Circuit Court, D.C.; Peter and

Southwick, *Cleveland Park*, pp. 17, 18; Bryan, *History of the National Capital*, p. 417; interview by the author with Priscilla McNeil, February 1989.

Page 51

The sale of Forrest Hill to President Grover Cleveland was made through Albert A. Wilson and Virginia Wilson, his wife, on May 26, 1886, D.C. Office of the Recorder of Deeds, Liber 1179, fol. 392, The price was $21,500. Twenty-eight acres are described in the deed. The sale of Oak View by Cleveland to Senator Francis G. Newlands was made April 21, 1890, D.C. Office of the Recorder of Deeds, Liber 1466, fol. 445. The price was $135,000. Twenty-six acres are described in the deed, with the same bounds as the 28 acres Cleveland originally purchased.

Page 54

The will of Ann Forrest Green reveals her attitude toward slavery and the South: "It is my will and desire that all the slaves I may die possessed of be free as they respectively reach the age of 35" and if the heirs are forced to sell that "none of my servants be sent further south than the District of Columbia and its immediate neighbors."

After President and Mrs. Cleveland, Red Top had a series of owners beginning with Senator Newlands. In 1928, Mr. and Mrs. Cazenove Lee bought Red Top and its remaining acreage. The Lees demolished the old house and on a site on Newark Street built an impressive brick Georgian colonial, using stone from Forrest Hill for steps, walls, and driveways. Cazenove Lee was a direct descendant of the Lee family of Virginia.

Page 57

The bronze statue of Pan, created by sculptress Edith Barretto Parsons, was presented to the Cathedral by the Faulkners. It was placed on the Cathedral grounds at the entrance of the Herb Cottage next to the Bishop's Garden, where it may be seen today. Mrs. Elizabeth Faulkner once commented to the author that its presence there was charming, "a delightful pagan touch" in the shadow of the great Cathedral.

Page 59

The founder of the firm that designed the Cathedral School Dormitories was architect Avery Faulkner, elder son of Mr. and Mrs. Waldron Faulkner.

Index

Adams, John, 34, 38
Addison, Thomas, 37
Addition to the Rock of Dumbarton, 7
Alexandria County, 75
Allegany County, 31

Balch, Rev. Thomas Bloomer, 44
Bank of Columbia, 31
Bankruptcy Act, 1800, 36, 75
Beall, George, 7, 68
Beall, Ninian, 7, 8
Beall, Samuel, Jr., 7
Beall's Lot, 7
Belt, Thomas Spriggs, 39, 40
Black, Elizabeth Matthews, 69, 71, 77
Black Squirrels, 69
Bohrer, Dr. Benjamin, 49
Boundary Street. See Florida Avenue
Brady, Michael, 39
Brightwood, 42
Brown, Flora, 54, 55
Brown, William Murphy, 54
Bulgarian Socialist Republic, 59
Burnett, Charles, 40
Burr, Aaron, 34, 74

Cathedral-Rosedale Neighborhood Committee, 59
Cathedral School. See National Cathedral School for Girls
Chesapeake and Ohio Canal, 55
Chesapeake Bay, 4
Churches: Christian Scientist (Church of Christ, Scientist), 56; National Cathedral (Cathedral of St. Peter and St. Paul), 57, 59; Presbyterian Meetinghouse, 44; St. Alban's, 53, 55; St. Ann's, 51; St. John's, 42
Circuit Court, District of Columbia, 38, 42, 47
City Lots. See Federal City Lots
Cleveland, Grover, 51, 54, 79
Cleveland, Frances Folsom (Mrs. Grover Cleveland), 51
Cleveland Park, 1, 54, 55, 61, 69
Cleveland Park Boundaries, 67
Cleveland Park Community Library Committee, 59
Cleveland Park, Development, 1, 8, 55, 59

Cleveland Park, First House Tour, 59
Colonial Land Grants, Patents, 1, 7
Commissioners, District, 4, 33, 35-37
Congress of the United States, 5, 31, 35, 36, 75, 76
Connecticut Avenue, 7, 54, 55
Coonley, Avery, 55, 56, 71
Coonley, Elizabeth (Mrs. Waldron Faulkner), 56, 71
Coonley, Queene Ferry (Mrs. Avery Coonley), 55, 56, 71
Cottage, the, 5, 6, 8, 9, 11, 13, 15, 16

Darnell, Henry, 7
Deakins, William, Jr., 5, 7, 8, 68
Decatur, Commodore Stephen, 49
Devereaux, Maria Green, 1, 28
District of Columbia. See Federal District
District of Columbia Medical Society, 42
Duvall, William, 40

Eastern Branch, 4, 75
Ellicott, Andrew, 33

Falls Street. See M Street
Faulkner, Avery, 59, 80
Faulkner, Celia (Celia Clevenger), 58
Faulkner, Elizabeth Coonley (Mrs. Waldron Faulkner), 56, 57, 71, 80
Faulkner, Waldron, 57, 71, 80
Faulkner, Winthrop, 57, 59, 71
Faulkner, Fryer & Vanderpool, 59
Federal City (City of Washington, National Capital), 1, 4, 7, 17, 28, 31-36, 38, 47, 67, 75, 78
Federal City Lots, 4, 36
Federal District (District of Columbia, Territory of Columbia), 1, 8, 38, 54, 67, 75
Fitzhugh, William Peregrine, 34
Florida Avenue, 54, 75
Flying Camp, Maryland, 2
Folsom Place. See 34th Place
Forrest, Ann (Mrs. John Green), 32, 48, 49, 79
Forrest, Benjamin Stoddert, 5, 32, 49
Forrest, Elizabeth (Mrs. Upton Read), 2, 5, 32, 49

Index

Forrest, George Plater, 32, 41, 49
Forrest, Henrietta Raley (Mrs. Thomas Forrest), 2
Forrest, Henry, 32
Forrest, Joseph, 32, 42
Forrest, Maria (Mrs. John Tayloe; Mrs. Benjamin Bohrer), 32, 49
Forrest, Rebecca Plater (Mrs. Uriah Forrest): courtship and marriage, 1, 2; death, 49; executrix, 47, 78; family and heritage, 1, 2, 32, 33, 49; gardens, 28, 30, 37; mistress of Rosedale, 17-28, 41, 42; pension, 48; residences, 1, 2, 4-6, 11, 13, 17, 28, 48, 49, 71, 72, 79; will, 49
Forrest, Richard, 32
Forrest, Thomas, 2,
Forrest, Uriah: amputation, health problems, 1, 2, 30, 34, 35, 37, 41, 42, 45, 77; bankruptcy, marshal's sale, 36, 37, 75, 78; builder, landholder, 1, 2, 5, 7, 8, 13, 17, 31, 32, 36, 67, 68, 78; business and commercial enterprises, 1, 2, 4, 31-34, 36, 74, 75; courtship and marriage, 1, 2; death and funeral, 42-45, 47, 76; family and heritage, 1, 2, 32, 33, 36, 49; military career, 1, 2, 31, 33, 35; politics, 33, 34; proprietor, federal city, 1, 4, 35, 36; public offices, 1, 4, 5, 38, 42; residences, 1, 2, 4, 59; will, 42, 47, 77
Forrest, Zachariah, 32
Forrest, Zephaniah, 32
Forrest & Stoddert, 2, 4, 32, 67, 68
Forrest Hill, 53, 79
Forrest-Marbury House (Forrest house, Georgetown), 2, 4, 5, 33, 67
Forrest, Stoddert and Murdock, 67
Fort Reno, 51
Frederick Street. See 34th Street, Georgetown
Friends of Rosedale, 61
Frost, John, 42

Gannon, James, 40
Generes, Monsieur, 40
Georgetown, 1, 2, 4-6, 8, 17, 33, 34, 41, 42, 44, 48, 75, 76
Georgetown Bridge Company, 31

Georgetown to Frederick Road. See Wisconsin Avenue
Georgetown Weekly Ledger, 74
Germantown, Battle of, 2, 45
Gift, the, 7
Grafton Apartments, 55
Green, Alice (Mrs. Angelo Iturbide), 51
Green, Ann Forrest (Mrs. John Green), 48, 49, 51, 54, 79
Green, George, 51
Green, John, 49
Greenleaf, James, 36, 75
Greenwood, 32
Guy Mason Center, 8

Halcyon House, 5
Half Pone Point, 32
Hamilton, Alexander, 34, 74
Harper, William, 38
Hearst, Playground, 54
Hepplewhite, George, 71
High Street, (Wisconsin Avenue, Georgetown), 44
Highlands The (Sidwell Friends School), 16, 54
Hooe, Robert Townsend, 38

Indians, 6, 7, 11, 69
Iturbide, Alice Green (Mrs. Angelo Iturbide), 51
Iturbide, Augustine, 51
Iturbide, Don Angelo, 51
Iturbide, Don Augustine, 51

Jay, John, 35
Jefferson, Thomas, 6, 38, 69, 74
Justice of the Peace, 38

Kent, James, 6, 69
Key, Elizabeth Plater (Mrs. Philip Barton Key), 33
Key, Francis Scott, 33
Key, Louisa (Mrs. Hatley Norton), 55
Key, Philip Barton, 33, 36, 47, 78
King, Adam & Co., 40
King, William, 44

Law, Thomas, 34, 37
Lear, Tobias, 6, 34, 69
Lee, Mr. and Mrs. Casanove, 52, 79

Index

Lee, Thomas Sim, 34, 37
L'Enfant, Pierre Charles, 6, 28, 33, 69
Lingan, Ann (Mrs. Thomas Plater), 32
Lingan, James, 32, 36
Linnean Hill, 8
Lord Baltimore, 7
Lot sales. See Federal City Lots
Lowndes, Charles, 37
Lowndes, Francis, 37
Lowndes, Rebecca (Mrs. Benjamin Stoddert), 5, 68, 74
Lucky Discovery, 7

M Street (Falls Street), 2, 4, 35, 44
Madison, Dolley (Mrs. James Madison), 49
Madison, James, 38, 49
Main, Thomas, 39
Marbury, William, 38, 68
Marbury v. Madison, 38
March, J., 39
Maryland Assembly, 4, 5
Maryland Gazette, 45
Maryland Loans, 36-38, 78
Mason, John, 4, 34
Massachusetts Avenue, 7, 54
Matthews, Ann Forrest, 69, 71, 76, 77
Maximilian, Emperor, 51
Mayor of Georgetown, 4, 36, 42
Melvin Hazen Park, 7
Midnight Judges, 38
Montgomery County, 1, 7, 32
Montrose Park, 8
Morris-Nicholson Syndicate, 35, 36, 75
Morris, Robert, 34-36, 75
Murdock, John, 67, 74
McGruder, Dr. Ninian, 36
McNeil, Priscilla, 7

National Cathedral (Cathedral of St. Peter and St. Paul), 59, 79
National Cathedral School for Girls, 59, 80
National Intelligencer and Washington Advertiser, 37, 42, 71
National Register of Historic Places, 1, 61, 67
National Zoo (National Zoological Park), 7, 8
Naval Observatory, 7, 54

Newlands, Senator Francis G., 54, 79
Nicholson, John, 35, 36, 75
Norton, Louisa Key (Mrs. Hatley Norton), 55
Norton Place, 55
Nourse, Charles, 54

Oak Hill Cemetery, 76
Oak View, 53, 79
Old Stone House, Georgetown, 8
Olmstead, Frederick Law, 54
Ordway Street, 57

P Street, 8
Pan, bronze statue, 57, 79
Patuxent River, 4, 17
Pension Act for Widows of War Veterans, 48
Peter, Grace Dunlap, 59
Philadelphia, City of, 5
Piedmont Plateau, 6
Pierce, Isaac, 39, 40
Pierce Mill Road. See Tilden Street
Pierce's Mill, 8, 55
Plater, Elizabeth (Mrs. Philip Barton Key), 33
Plater, Elizabeth Rousby (Mrs. George Plater III), 1, 2
Plater, George III, 1
Plater, George IV, 32
Plater, George V, 49
Plater, John, 32
Plater, Rebecca. See Rebecca Plater Forrest
Plater, Thomas, 32
Potomac River, 2, 4, 6-8, 69
Presbyterian Burial Ground, 44, 49, 76
Presbyterian Meetinghouse, 44
Pretty Prospects (Pretty Prospect), 5-8, 54, 68
Privateers, Pro-French American, 5
Proprietors, Federal City 1, 35, 36
Prospect Street, 5

Quarries, 6, 7
Quern, 28, 72

Ramsay, Dennis, 38
Read, Elizabeth Forrest, and Upton Read, 49

Index

Red Top, 53, 54, 79
Redwood, 32
Reintzell, Daniel, 36
Residence Bill, 4, 35
Riggs of Georgetown, 40
Riverside, Illinois, 56
Roads and Streets, references to:
  Albemarle Street, 7; Highland Place, 55; Macomb Street, 51; Newark Street, 51, 55, 59, 79; 34th Street, Cleveland Park 55; 36th Street, 59
Rock Creek, 6-8, 11, 54, 55
Rock of Dumbarton, 7
Rolling Road, 4, 69
Rosedale, Entrance Gate, cover, 39, 41, 44, 76
Rosedale Estate: accessory buildings and equipment, 30, 57; cottage, 5, 6, 8, 9, 11, 15, 16; farm, 28, 30, 39, 40, 49; furnishings, 17-28; gardens, 28, 30, 37, 56, 57; ghosts, 61; livestock, 30, 37, 39, 57; marshal's sale, 37; office, 23, 39; ownership: Forrest, Green and heirs, 5, 13, 48, 49, 56; Coonley, Faulkner and heirs, 55-57; National Cathedral, 57, 59; Youth for Understanding, 59; residence, 13, 55, 56, 59, 71
Rosedale, Name of, 67

St. Mary's County, 1, 2, 32, 34, 38, 68
Seward, Secretary of State William, 51
Sherman, John, 55
Sidwell Friends School, 54
Smith's, Mrs., Boarding School, 40
Sons of the American Revolution, 76
Sotterley Manor, 2, 4, 11, 17, 32, 34, 41, 68
Southwick, Joyce D., 59
Stoddert, Benjamin, 5, 7, 8, 37, 68, 74
Stoddert, Benjamin Forrest, 68
Stoddert, Rebecca Lowndes (Mrs. Benjamin Stoddert), 5, 68, 74
Suter's Tavern, 4, 68

Taverns: Barney's, 37; Suter's, 4, 68; Union, 34
Tayloe, John, 49
Templeman, John, 78

Tenleytown, 49, 51, 69
Tenleytown Public Elementary School, 55
Territory of Columbia. See Federal District
Thirty Fourth Place (Folsom Place), 53, 55
Thirty Fourth Street, Georgetown (Frederick Street), 2, 4
Thornton, Anna Maria Brodeau (Mrs. William Thornton), 32, 34, 72
Thornton, Dr. William, 32, 34
Threlkeld, John, 37, 42
Tilden Street (Pierce Mill Road), 55
The, Gift, 7
Tidewater Maryland, 1, 2, 4
Tobacco, 2

Uptown Theater, 7

War: Civil, 51; 1812, 49; 1793, 5, 35; Revolutionary, 2, 5, 33, 34, 45
Washington County, 38, 75
Washington, D.C. See Federal City
Washington, George, 2, 4, 33, 68, 71, 74
Washington, Martha Custis (Mrs. George Washington), 34
Way, A. and G., 39
Welsh, Bromwell and Ruth, 40
West, Georgia Green, 71
Wilson, Albert A. and Virginia, 79
Wisconsin Avenue, 6-8, 32, 41, 44, 54, 55, 69
Woodley, (Maret School, Woodley Oaks), 16, 33
Woodley Lane (Woodley Road), 32, 51, 55
Worthington, Dr. Charles, 41, 42, 76
Wright, Frank Lloyd, 16, 56

Young, Notley, 34
Youth for Understanding, 59, 61

Zantzinger, Isabel Green, 34, 74